Pitman
Education
Library

Drama and the Teacher

Drama and the teacher

Drama
and the Teacher

DEREK BOWSKILL

Pitman Publishing

First published 1974

Sir Isaac Pitman and Sons Ltd
Pitman House, Parker Street, Kingsway,
London WC2B 5PB
PO Box 46038, Banda Street, Nairobi, Kenya

Sir Isaac Pitman (Aust.) Pty Ltd
Pitman House, 158 Bouverie Street, Carlton,
Victoria 3053, Australia

Pitman Publishing Corporation
6 East 43rd Street, New York, NY 10017, USA

Sir Isaac Pitman (Canada) Ltd
495 Wellington Street West, Toronto 135,
Canada

The Copp Clark Publishing Company
517 Wellington Street West, Toronto 135,
Canada

Text set in 10/11 pt. IBM Journal Roman,
printed by photolithography,
and bound in Great Britain at The Pitman Press,
Bath.

G.4673/4674:15

Preface

There is no mystique to the teaching of drama. Its special skills are only an extension of those needed every day in the ordinary class-room.

This book makes clear and plain the place of drama and dramatic method and balances any necessary philosophizing with an abundance of exercises typifying approaches to classroom work. The exercises are all exemplary and can easily be adapted to meet individual needs of students, pupils and teachers. There is no need for any of the exercises to be slavishly followed. It is hoped that many of them will appeal as they stand, but it is equally hoped that readers will adapt them freely to suit their special circumstances. The wealth of typical exercises in the book is a key to the method recommended — direct, physical participation.

Drama may begin in the world of the imagination but it becomes alive and effective only if a frontal attack is made on those involved. Its benefits can be seen in the growth of directness, sensitivity and sensibility in thought, feeling, speech and movement — in brief, in self-awareness and self-confidence.

The following chapters outline this growth with ideas appropriate to the pupils' stage of development. Basically it is a one-way move-ment, but it must allow two-way variations at every stage. The main stages are given below. Each one is the subject of a separate chapter:

1 Sensing and perceiving.
2 Making responses.
3 Practising skills.
4 Organizing and manipulating.
5 Enriching.

6   Sharing.
7   Performing.

In the final resort, all drama is about here-and-now, person-to-person experiences. Rich and significant drama is about frank explorations of non-rigid relationships.

It is hoped this book will help stimulate genuine responses and fresh pronouncements in the pursuit of drama — the imaginative communication of significant experience.

I would like to thank Celia Randall for her kind permission to use her poem, and Ronnie Duncan for the extracts from his play, as well as for all the knowing sympathy, encouragement and inspiration he has given freely over the years.

For the drawings of the pin-men, and for the photographs, I accept full responsibility.

I would like to offer this book in dedication as a tribute and token to my companions in Devon — Where I taught so little and learned so much — wherever they now may be.

Derek Bowskill

Contents

1

Where to Begin?
(Sensing and Perceiving)

WORKING FROM ONE'S CENTRE

If drama is to achieve a meaningful place in pupils' lives it must start in situations and conditions they can easily recognize and occupy. A crucial condition is that they must be relaxed and at ease in their roles — crucial because otherwise the latent forces of dramatic expression will not begin to stir. Creativity and imagination do not flourish when pupils are nervous about their task or unsure of their self-images. Their tasks must contain sufficient elements they fully understand for their interest to be caught. They must be secure and comfortable in their self-images so they can relax and free-wheel into practical work. The combination of understanding and security will create a beginning position that is clear and steady — desirable since journey and destination alike are unknown when the activity is creative and imaginative.

It is no good, however, *telling* pupils not to be shy or hesitant; not to cover up or block. Drama is made up of dreams — personal and private hopes and fears — and none of us will confess or express them unless we are secure and confident in surroundings and atmosphere. We must not only be prepared for personal release — we must also know and feel (belly-know and belly-feel) that we are. The self-images must be appropriate.

It may appear possible to command pupils to "sit up and be taught" in those tightly structured situations sometimes considered proper for academic subjects. (How much they *actually learn* under such conditions is debatable and not central to this chapter.) But pupils cannot be forced into creativity. Unless they are relaxed and self-determined, the barriers will be up and much energy, skill and

1

affection will be needed to bring them down. The range of personal
anxieties that send up the barriers is wide: there is the inarticulate
boy who thinks he will be made to "utter"; the country boy who
thinks he will be made to speak differently; the gang-leader who
does not wish to lose face by being "cissy"; the girl who is worried
she may show her knickers; the girl who does not wish to draw
attention to her bitten fingernails; the boy or girl who is never
comfortable until out of school uniform. These are typical personal
anxieties that can prohibit expressive, dramatic work.

It is, of course, possible to coerce responses from unwilling
pupils. But the responses will be conditioned-reflex actions rather
than personal testimonies. They will be clichés designed to protect
the pupil from personal engagement of his private spirit. When the
clichés fail to satisfy, everyone becomes frustrated and tense. (The
exercise may be repeated!) When the clichés succeed a monument
is erected to hyprocrisy and deceit. Trust is lost and pupil and
teacher are driven further apart.

Pupils can only work creatively from their *real personal inner
condition.* The sympathetic teacher knows this and goes out to
meet hesitant pupils, since it is probably not their fault that they
are so. I have known many teachers in training who were anxious
and hesitant about what they felt were poor and fumbling attempts
at creativity, simply because, when young, they had had little
opportunity to experiment *without the fear of failure* or the *worry
of the comparative comments* that would inexorably end the exercise.

When a pupil has exposed his inner self comparisons are
irrelevant. They *can* be dangerous. If the comparison is "favourable"
it may set up values that will encourage the wrong kind of pride
and competition. If the comparison is not "favourable," it will
not encourage the child to do better but will distort proper signs
of personal shyness. Hesitancies are only removed by trust. The
pupil must be, and feel, free from all worry about standards,
achievements and improvement. There must be no overtone
of right or wrong; good or bad; failure or success. Neither the
earliest nor the latest flowerings of the creative human spirit are
susceptible to such judgements.

I remember vividly a visit I made as an LEA adviser to a small
village school. A speech lesson was in full progress and I was

invited to watch. The children were performing party pieces. I could see no enjoyment in any face except that of the teacher — for the rest it seemed like a dreadful initiation ceremony. It came the turn of a girl who was particularly hesitant. General attention was drawn to her anxiety and my particular attention was requested so that I could bear witness to "how badly she spoke." The following then occurred. Teacher to child "Go on. Say something. Let Mr Bowskill hear how badly you speak. Go on. Speak up." The child managed to mutter a few words before crumpling into tears. She was sent to her place and the incident was closed — for the teacher. The child was five years old.

Such insensitivity can only inhibit those active and direct responses which are central to buoyant learning situations. In creative work they are quintessential.

CONCENTRATION AND ABSORPTION

The responses need the support of keenly developed powers of concentration and absorption if the potential of the learning situation is to be fully exploited.

Concentration is under the *control* of the individual will while absorption, which may grow out of concentration, comes, more like virtue, as something *given*. Concentration is a self-conscious state in which we activate our attention and *positively* search. Absorption is a non-conscious state in which we surrender attention and *passively* become lost.

One of the best ways to train pupils' powers of concentration is to aid their absorption — to encourage it and work from it; to respect it and not undermine or destroy it — no matter what its focus may be. The nearer any task is to a pupil's personal interests, the narrower will be the gap between (necessary) concentration and (desirable) absorption and the more he will be prepared to bridge it voluntarily.

USING THE SENSES: EXPERIENCE — EXPRESSION — COMMUNICATION

There is little possibility of absorption and less purpose in concentration if the pupil is not using his major senses properly. He will be denied awareness of the necessary physical stimuli — sensation — and also the ability to interpret them — perception.

Creativity flowers when an absorbed and concentrating pupil's receptors (eyes, ears, nose, etc.) are sensitively tuned to *detect change.* Then he can perceive their messages, draw conclusions and imagine possibilities.

The combination of:

> being absorbed and concentrating;
> receiving sensations;
> perceiving messages;
> drawing conclusions; and
> imagining possibilities

constitutes our inner experience.

Creative drama consists of three stages:

> Enriching the inner experience.
> Encouraging its expression.
> Stimulating its communication.

These three stages aid the pupil's progress to:

> Self-awareness of internal experience.
> Flexibility of personal expression.
> Success in communication.

A pupil's ability to sense experience, express it eloquently (kinetically and/or vocally) and communicate it efficiently will be fostered if the experiences contain rich and significant material — *rich and significant to pupil and teacher in terms that both can validate.*

The fostering depends upon two main factors:

> The quality of the stimuli.
> The receptivity of the pupil.

Occupying a central position is the *efficiency of the pupils' sensory mechanisms.* Everything we experience comes through our senses and we can learn nothing if they are numbed or blocked.

It is extraordinary how little attention is paid to the education of the senses when the rest of the educational process depends upon them absolutely. Many pupils go through their school lives looking without seeing; listening without hearing, and touching without feeling. Efforts should be made to correct the situation, since efficiency alone would justify it — never mind improving the aesthetics of living. (Oscar Wilde was quite right to suggest it was a good thing that art education in England was poor — otherwise we would rush from class and tear down our buildings!)

Young people who are aware of the power of their senses and able to use them perceptively and well are lucky indeed. Most pupils will need some kind of help to get started. The exercises at the end of the chapter will help them towards a lasting interest in using their senses to the full. The order is arbitrary. The aim is to offer each pupil an intriguing and engaging starting point where *he is at ease.* There is no exercise that cannot be tackled by "beginner" or "expert" and each is directly relevant to everyday life. The exercises will probably work best if they *appear* to arise accidentally rather than be made the subject of a lesson. Once enthusiasm has begun, special times can be set aside. In the early stages, it is best to use the exercises little and often, making few, if any, overt references to their purpose. *The more the teacher can identify with the exercises at a level of enjoyed, personal commitment the more effectively will they work.*

EXERCISES
(All the exercises can be undertaken individually, in pairs, in groups or as a full class.)

Looking and Seeing
1 The pupils find all the blemishes and mistakes on any single page in a textbook — especially intriguing when the books are new. They share their discoveries — discussing patterns or blemishes they like personally.

2 The pupils find inkstains (or other marks) in textbooks or exercise books (preferably not their own). They try to find examples of the following: birds, men, houses, ships, chimneys, spiders, etc. They discuss what they find informally with one another. They write *detailed* descriptions of what they have found.

From one another's descriptions of what they have found they recreate the chosen shape. They write about and discuss what they *felt about* the shapes they found.

They find a scratch or mark on a desk or chair that looks like one of the inkstains. Then they find one on the walls, ceiling or floor.

3*(a)*   The pupils look at the patterns of lines on their hands until they can see one of the things from 2.

3*(b)*   They make them into railway lines and points; or a contour map — giving names to the valleys and mountains.

3*(c)*   They look at their hands until they find something that is *genuinely new* — something never seen there before.

4*(a)*   The pupils find a feature on their hand that particularly interests them — a nail; a mark; a hair. They look at it until they see nothing but that special feature — aware of *nothing else* — "lost" in it.

4*(b)*   Repeat with any of the objects from the previous exercises and generally extend the exercise (looking with maximum concentration) until sight is the only sense being used — excluding hearing and touch in particular. All the concentration will be focused upon looking at the chosen object(s).

5   Repeat exercises 1-4 with a partner so that *discoveries* are shared, seen and talked about.

6   The pupils look at part of the room for x minutes. They close their eyes and recall it in the mind. They open eyes to check for accuracy of recall. Repeat with different parts of the room. Cut down on x as soon as possible until the exercise works with only a glance.

(The selected part of the room should be no more than four feet square — one square foot may be sufficient at first — most pupils can work freely within 2 x 2 ft to 4 x 1 ft.)

7*(a)*   Repeat 6, but instead of recalling it in the mind describe it to a partner who has eyes open and is looking at it.

7*(b)*   Repeat *(a)* — using hands in the air to draw, paint or sculpt the chosen area.

8   Repeat 7*(b)* but make the drawing, painting or sculpting real. (It will probably be best if the selected area for recall is in another space — removed from the room where the painting is to be done. The hall or corridor outside should be enough to prevent or discourage "chance" sight.)

9   Give the pupils photographs, sketches or line-drawings of people, animals and things represented naturalistically or in an abstract style. The pupils look until they can "see" other things, animals or people beginning to grow.

Examples of some black and white visuals that can quickly help tap the pupils' imagination and sub-conscious are given on the following pages (colour prints and slides can be used equally effectively). The following questions typify one way of encouraging responses:

> What is it? or Who is it? or What are they?
> Where is it? What is happening?
> Is it coming or going? Is it moving or still?
> What has just happened? What is to happen next?
> What is it thinking . . . feeling . . . saying?
> What does it look like? What does it remind you of?
> What does it make you think of? Do you like it?
> Can you see a ——? (object suggested by the teacher)
> What is this? (small part of the visual)
> What do you feel about it?

10 One of the pupils stands in a position he chooses for himself (perhaps a "special" position — but not too difficult). He keeps absolutely still. The rest of the pupils concentrate on his body shape. Sketches are made by the pupils of the body shape. If possible, Polaroid photographs are taken. Another pupil then recreates the shape assumed by the first. The rest of the pupils comment on the accuracy of the reproduction. Changes may be suggested or made — by the pupil himself and/or the others — to improve accuracy. The sketches and/or photographs are produced for further comment and/or change.

There can be keen interest in the *exact* position of an eyebrow or a finger and concentration and observation can trigger lively discussion of the *body shape itself* (objective) as well as its *meaning* (subjective). Needless to say, the exercise requires an atmosphere of trust and friendly relaxation. It is an event that should be co-operative not competitive.

11 The pupils imagine in their mind's eye an entirely new colour. They describe and discuss with a partner and together write descriptions. (The end product of this exercise is not important — efforts, process and side-effects give it its merit. The exercises should not be used until powers of concentration have been well built up in the class.)

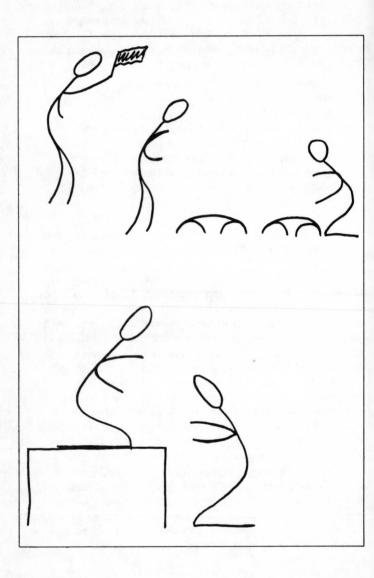

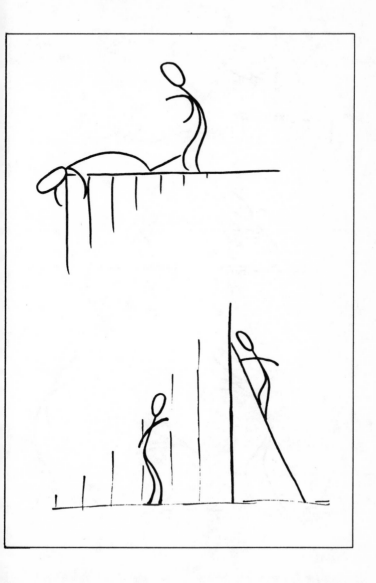

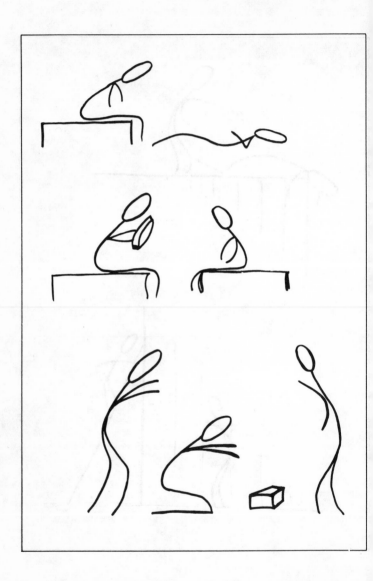

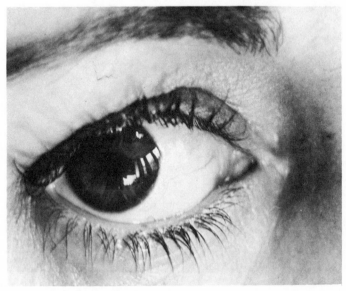

12 In groups of six to eight, give the pupils a lemon, a potato or a matchstick each. Let them study it for as long as they wish. Replace in a container, "shuffle" and let them find their original.

13 Play the "Objects on a Tray" memory game. (This game is used for a number of the senses. On each occasion accuracy of memory can be stressed or relaxed dependent upon need. In the early stages it is good to separate quantity from quality — remembering them all *vaguely* or a *few accurately*. The pupils need not know your priority every time.)

Touching

1 The pupils find different textures in the room — as many as possible. They feel them first with the tips of the fingers and later with (for example) nose, cheeks, inner wrist, elbow.

2 The pupils make journeys over the school premises, indoors and out, in bare feet. This can be extended to work in pairs — one of the partners with eyes firmly closed. (It is important to decide whether talking should be allowed or not. Conversation with a partner *changes the nature of the experience.* It might be wise to let the pupils know they are going to try the exercise twice — the first time with no talking. The experiences come to the "blind" partner intensely.) If it is not appropriate for a journey to be made round the school, different surfaces can be prepared within the classroom: rough hessian cloth; smooth silky cloth; wet cloth; dry sandpaper, wet sandpaper; sand, soil, pebbles and water in trays. Some pupils may wish to try a journey from home to school barefoot.

3(*a*) The pupils walk over and/or touch with the toes and feet one of the surfaces from 2 above. They concentrate on this to the exclusion of everything else — as in 4 (*a*) in "Looking and Seeing."

3(*b*) They concentrate until they are aware of *nothing* but toe or foot.

3(*c*) They *become* the foot or the toe.

(These are excellent starters for storytelling or writing. Descriptions of what was experienced; where pupils thought they were; and what they felt can be lively and far-reaching.) Eyes can be open or closed — if both are to be tried they should be closed first and open second.

4   Give the pupils a stone, pebble, piece of driftwood or coal. Let them handle it with eyes closed for as long as they wish. Take it away. They then:

(i)   describe it to a partner;

(ii)   draw or paint it.

5(a)   In pairs, with eyes closed, pupils feel the hand of their partner. With the free hand sketch in the air, largely, a detailed portrait of the hand. Since the pupils are working simultaneously with their partners it is a useful exercise in personal sensitivity. (At whatever stage of development the exercise is introduced, time will be needed to absorb the social energy and the rise in emotional temperature. The atmosphere should be allowed to subside naturally. If it is too difficult for partners to work simultaneously, start one only with eyes closed "painting in the air" and bring in the partner as soon as possible.)

5(b)   When ready, repeat (a), but this time using the face of the partner.

6   With the eyes closed handle a variety of fresh vegetables. Describe and discuss them with a partner.

7   Play the "Donkey's Tail" game with as many variations of object and attachment as possible. Then progress to making simple models; three-dimensional building "toys"; paper sculpture; feathers and glue; finger paints; etc. There will be a contrast between the objects the pupils think they are making — especially in collage work — and what they see when they open their eyes. This contrast will encourage language flow and group discussion. It may manifest itself in an explosion of social energy. This should be recognized for what it is: the need to communicate when in the presence of the unexpected. Be prepared!

8   Use colour supplements, or equivalent, to make a collage. When the collages are well begun, ask the pupils to choose the most satisfying or effective pieces and collect them together. These pieces are then *thrown away*. The pupils complete the collage by touch only, using the materials left over.

9   Play the "Objects on a Tray" game with the eyes closed using only the sense of touch.

10 Use the exercises 1-4 from "Looking and Seeing," substituting touch for sight.

11 In groups of five or six, the pupils sit in a circle sharing a piece of cloth — large enough for everyone to hold it with both hands. Begin with the exploration of texture. Eyes should be closed throughout the exercise. When the pupils have settled they talk about what they are touching and what they think and feel about it — a personal monologue about what they *feel* about the texture of the cloth — not a description of it. The voice level should enable everyone to hear the rest without undue effort. It is not group discussion but members of a group, speaking personally, out loud, all together. From the group will come a "symphony" of words and sentences related to the cloth and united by it. The pupils should concentrate mainly on the touching of the cloth and what they are thinking and feeling about it. (It is important that the pupils do not see the cloth before they start the exercise nor should they open their eyes during it. At a later stage it will be possible for them to undertake the exercise with the eyes open yet still concentrating exclusively on the sense of touch. In the early stages it is wisest for eyes to be firmly closed.)

Listening

1 The pupils sit or stand as far apart as possible and listen to the sound of breathing — other pupils' first; then their own. When this is established they listen *for* the sound of their heart beating. (Follow this by listening *for* the sound of the blood as it moves through the body.)

2(*a*) The pupils stand in a number of different places at school, inside and out, and note all the different sounds they hear. Eyes closed.

2(*b*) They stand in one spot (eyes closed) and listen to the sounds. When they have a clear picture of the objects and people surrounding them they open eyes and check for accuracy.

2(*c*) They stand in the same spot and listen again — after a time open eyes and notice how the sounds appear to change with the opening of the eyes.

3 In pairs the pupils journey round the school, inside and out-

side — one partner leading, the other with eyes closed. No talking at all — just listening. They return to discuss with partners the journey they made.

4(a)   The pupils listen to a popular number from the current "hit parade," ignoring the main melody and beat and listening only for those sounds that lie beneath the surface.

4(b)   Repeat (a), accompanying the "hidden" sounds by tapping, humming or clicking fingers.

4(c)   Repeat (b) with a musical instrument. (It is probably best to use percussion at first.)

5   In groups of five or six let one pupil establish a time beat using the ideas from 4 above. When this is established, members of group join in and continue it. When this is established one or more of the group play *against* the beat of the group.

(Exercises 4 and 5 take time since it requires hard concentration for pupils to listen — exclusively and perceptively — to a particular sound.)

Smell

1   Just as the distinctive textures in the room were examined by the fingertips for their special *feel,* so now they should be examined for their special *smell* — tables, chairs, pipes, radiators, curtains and papers.

2(a)   The pupils identify objects, given by a partner, by their smell. (Eyes closed.)

2(b)   Repeat with domestic foods and drinks.

2(c)   Repeat with fresh vegetables. Later with all kinds of vegetable matter — fresh and decaying. (This particular exercise will be easier if the school is near open country — but most schools should be able to provide a contrast from trees, bushes, flowers and grass, etc.)

3   Play the "Objects on a Tray" game — using sponge pieces with different scents and perfumes. (Some should be the same.) All the sponges should look the same. The game can be played with eyes open and closed.

4   Repeat the exercises in "Listening" 1-3, substituting the sense of smell.

5   In pairs the pupils share a smell they enjoy. They describe

and discuss it with partner. The exercise can be tried with eyes
open or closed.

Taste
　1(*a*)　With eyes closed the pupils taste a piece of normal
domestic food and try to identify it. (The range is extensive —
from all kinds of sweets and fruits to cooked potatoes and other
vegetables.) There will probably be considerable discussion about
the taste with eyes open and eyes closed being different. The
sense of touch — the texture in the mouth — may remain the
same, but the taste will change, so:
　1(*b*)　Repeat: specially noticing the change in taste at the
moment of seeing what the food is.
　2　The pupils taste a number of fresh vegetables with eyes
open and closed. (This exercise can be related to those for touch
and smell. There is scope for description and discussion about
what taste is *expected* from the look and the feel — and the other
ways round.)
　3　Play the "margarine and butter" game. Follow by identifying "sandwich spreads."
　4(*a*)　The pupils identify the tastes of watered essences — it
can be played as an "Objects on a Tray" game.
　4(*b*)　Repeat with drinks made from the following: cold coffee
— with milk — with sugar — without; cold tea, milk, chocolate.
Change the temperatures. Use a little wine with a lot of water —
with no water — with a little — red and white mixed.
　5　Repeat any of the exercises 1-3. The pupils try, by
imagination and will-power, to *change the taste* with the food
still in the mouth.
　6(*a*)　The pupils recall tastes in their imagination. Check with
the real taste for accuracy.
　6(*b*)　Repeat but use a different taste to trigger the imaginary
one. Check for accuracy.

AUDIO-VISUAL AIDS TO SENSATION AND PERCEPTION
Most pupils live in homes where radios, TV sets, record-players and
tape-recorders are almost commonplace. They are surrounded by
the instruments (some would say infernal machines) of an age of

technology (some would say technocracy). Certainly refrigerators, vacuum-cleaners, motor-cars, mopeds, electric razors and tooth-brushes are no longer novelties and seen against a backcloth of space travel techniques their status is reduced to that of toys.

It is foolish not to draw upon these resources when and where-ever possible to help forward the pupils' work, and their under-standing and control of electronic-mechanical stimuli. If the pupils are to have proper control of their personal development they must be helped come to terms with the sound-and-light machines and techniques of contemporary society. The brains of commerce and entertainment wrest maximum impact from audio-visual aids. If education is to enable the pupils to make free choices and develop and fulfil their total personae, these aids must be integrated into the educational system and unless teachers can identify with the techniques (and their employment in our broad culture and the pupils' current sub-culture) they will not be helping pupils to withstand the impact of "future shock." Many teachers are worried about this identification — but an identification with techniques and cultures does not necessitate exclusive occupation. It guarantees experiences held in common — the only valid condi-tion out of which self-directed, co-operative learning can emerge.

The main aids available for educating sensation and perception fall into two main groups : sound and light.

Sound

If record-players and tape-recorders are to be used, the teacher should ensure (by patient rehearsal and practice if necessary) he has mastered the handling techniques and knows the machines. False starts, wrong volume levels, bad connections, inferior recordings and fumbling inefficiencies will annoy the pupils, frustrate imaginative creativity and defeat the purpose of using the aid. Until the handling is perfectly mastered, the machines are best left unused. (For example: if the volume is turned up when the stylus is lowered on to a record, there will be unnecessary noise and an abrupt start. The volume should be turned down — the stylus placed in the correct position — the volume turned to the desired level : simple, smooth and effective.)

Tape-recorders can be used to make useful sounds and/or music by teachers and/or pupils. Sound effects; abstract sound-tracks; music and vocalization can all be made and varied by dubbing and additive recordings; playing at different speeds and/or backwards; orthodox editing.

The addition of sound-generators and copy-cat-echo machines opens a world of experiment and exploration—happily uniting the creative and the scientific. (For example: the sound of breathing and tapping on a table—recorded close, possibly with echo added, and played back at double or half speed, provide intriguing and impelling sound stimuli.)

Class-made sounds and music help bring a sense of unity to the work and one of the main benefits of drama is to help pupils perceive the universal unity in the midst of apparent diversity—to achieve an understanding of the wholeness of things.

> There is in souls a sympathy with sounds;
> And, as the mind is pitch'd the ear is pleas'd
> With melting airs, or martial, brisk, or grave:
> Some chord in unison with what we hear
> Is touch'd within us, and the heart replies.[1]

There is, however, an important place for recorded music — classical or modern; abstract or programme. Pupils seem to respond best to the contemporary and the abstract, and their journeys into the world of music for drama should start there — where they identify— and move backwards historically. The following is a list of recorded music that speaks directly to the pupils and does not prompt cliché responses.

Music for Practical Work
Winter Music   Richard Rodney Bennett   Delta DEL 12005
(Classical idiom, highly stylized but not difficult)
The Miraculous Mandarin   Bela Bartok DG LPM 18873
(Modern classical idiom — strong rhythms, rich harmonics and many contrasts)
The Sound of a Bass François Rabbath Philips B 77973
(A number of highly individual pieces featuring a double-bass in

---

[1] *The Task* — "The Winter Walk at Noon," by William Cowper.

the modern classical idiom with strong rhythms and rich contrasts
Density and Other Pieces Edgar Varese Philips ABL 3392
(A strong combination of modern/classical orthodox music and
electronics)
Kilimanjaro and Other Pieces Miriam Makebe London HA 8111
London HA 2332
(African ethnic music translated into the pop idiom)
Hi-Fi Drums   Capitol T 926
(Rich, complex, contrasting pieces for percussion)
Still I'm Sad   Columbia D 137706
(Chant and plainsong in the pop idiom)
Persuasive Percussion   London HAZ 2357
(Simple contrasting rhythms in a sugary style)
Zeitmasse and Other Pieces Stockhausen Philips ABL 3386
(Offers many opportunities for solo work from the modern/
classical idiom)
Symphony No. 6 in C Sharp Minor Mahler CBS BRG 72182
(Rich orthodox/classical composition with strong contrasts)
Pictures at an Exhibition Mussorgsky Columbia 33CX 1421
Job   Vaughan Williams   Decca LXT 2937
(Both these suites offer great contrast in melodies, harmonies and
rhythms)
Musical Gems of the Twentieth Century   Supraphon SUA 10479
Evolution   Verv ULP 9014
Jazz Suite   EMI 33 SX 1774
Witches Brew   RCA RC 16156
Sounds of New Music   Folkways FX 6160
Concert Percussion   Time 58000 Series 2000
(The above collections all offer contrasts in style, rhythm and
melody from classical to current in pieces of varying lengths)
Disraeli Gears   Cream   Polydor 593 003
Fresh Cream   Cream   Polydor 593 001
Wheels of Fire   Cream   Polydor 583 033
(Music in the modern/classical/pop idiom from a well-known
group)
Black Marigolds   Michael Garrick   Argo ZDA 88
Dusk Fire   Michael Garrick   EMI SX 6064
The Heart is a Lotus   Michael Garrick   Argo ZDA 135

(Music in the modern/classical idiom but with a strong beat and marked melodies from a small jazz combination)

Kulu Se Mama	John Coltrane	HMV CLP 3617
Meditations	John Coltrane	HMV CLP 3575

(Complex and advanced rhythms and harmonies requiring deep concentration)

Vienna 1908-1914	Philips SAL 3539

(A useful cross-section of early music in the modern/classical idiom)

Instant Karma	Apple 1003
Bang-Bang	EMI LIB 66160
Give Peace a Chance	Apple 13
Jenny Take a Ride	EMI SS 481
A Whiter Shade of Pale	Decca DM 126
Ha-Ha Said the Clown	Fontana TF 812
Something's Burning	Pye RS 20888

(Selections from modish pop music — a highly subjective area, this; but the author has found all the above particularly exciting and worthwhile in class work)

The Seasons	BBC RESR 7

(A compilation of words and radiophonic music from the author's BBC radio programme "Drama Workshop")

Some "Top of the Pops" music achieves a permanency. Some, however, should be used only while it is popular and fashionable — either to add depth to the musical and dramatic experience or to expose superficiality.

Pre-recorded tapes for creative work in drama are now becoming easily available. ("Drama Workshop"[1] and "Workshop One"[2] are two.) While these tapes can be of great help in the early stages of practical work, they have the disadvantage held in common with the printed word — they achieve a concrete state in teachers' and pupils' minds and are frequently used unmodified and intact. They are only properly useful when edited and prepared (rearranged

---

[1] Recordings of this BBC programme are available from Stagesound (London) Ltd, 11/12 King Street, WC2E 8HU. Telephone 01—240 0955.

[2] "Workshop One" is published by J. M. Dent & Sons Ltd and is a stimulus kit of tape, film strip, pupils' books and teachers' book.)

and played backwards if need be) according to the pupils' needs.
They are not inviolate and the form should be given less respect
than it seems to require.

Whatever the audio aids, from a solitary cymbal to complex
amplifying systems, they do not achieve the impact and the
influence of the use of light.

Light

One of the most keenly powerful forces at the disposal of the
teacher, yet one of the most under-used, is light. Carefully
designed lighting can completely transform an otherwise un-
prepossessing environment so that it takes on a richer life, clothed
in atmosphere. Society at large uses light to influence us at every
turn — shops, supermarkets, restaurants, churches, bingo halls,
youth clubs and discothèques — yet there are few schools where
even the beginnings have been made.

Human responses to colour and particularly to coloured light
are emotionally powerful and very subjective but, *in general
terms only,* the following seems to apply:

Warm colours appear to move towards the viewer — advancing.
Cold colours appear to move away from the viewer —
retreating.
Reds and Oranges are powerful and strong; assertive and
aggressive — warm.
Yellows are stimulating, happy and cheerful.
Blues and Greens are cool, quiet and restful.
Purples are regal and grand; strong and assertive.
White stimulates — Black depresses — Grey neutralizes.

EXERCISES

Here are one or two ways in which the pupils' interest may be
gained without resource to expensive equipment.

Best is a fully-blacked-out space but an effective dim-out can
be achieved by draping some, if not all, of the windows with
dyed sacking, inexpensive black hessian, cotton rayon or rep.
Black sugar-paper, brown paper or even newspaper and sticky
tape will create helpful dimming — particularly on winter after-
noons. The dim-out can easily be arranged to allow a few rays of

sunlight through and these will provide a basis for pupils to explore texture, colour and shadow. The following are introductions to the idea:

(a)   Placing a lighted match or candle in the direct rays of the sun and contrasting the effect in the shadow; placing the hands in the direct rays so that the apparent shape is different from usual — perhaps concentrating on the hairs on the hand — noticing high- lighting and shadow; moving the hands slowly, pivoting them, in the beam of light so that changes in appearance and shadow are made clear and plain.

(b)   Placing any three-dimensional object in the direct beam so that its nature and shape appear different; choosing objects with this exercise in mind and forecasting the changes; arranging a desk (and/or chair, etc.) in the direct beam and concentrating on one aspect until it appears to grow into something different; using hands in these arrangements of desk/chair to control shadow and texture or to add to meaning; placing the flat surface of a desk or chair in the rays so that all the previously overlooked scratches, blemishes, curves, etc., become noticeable and, as a result of con- centration, take on a life of their own.

(c)   Placing the hands in the beams of the sunlight but inter- posing coloured filters so the flesh becomes tinted; using the coloured filters to project on to the face, or part of a face — eyes, ears, nose and mouth; placing paintings and pieces of sculpture — especially blanched wood, polystyrene or plaster of paris — in the beams and interposing coloured filters. (The exercises will be dramatically effective if objects and filters are primary colours.)

Another simple introductory step can be made with small groups working in a store cupboard, if no other blacked-out space is available. They can work with inexpensive light-boxes used in science laboratories. Small objects can be made to appear distorted in the coloured beams of light from mirrors and prisms, etc.

In the same small space — or in the classroom or hall, provided the blackout is good enough — use can be made of the standard film-strip or slide projectors, episcope and epidiascopes. They all throw a single narrow beam (the essence of work on light, colour and shade) and combine the facility of projecting slides, strips, photographs, paintings, etc. The single beam can be used in the ways already suggested for sunlight as well as the following:

(a)   Use a wide-angle lens so that even in a confined space it will be possible to project a large image to enable the shape, form and colour to be most effective. Provided the size is right there is no need for fine focus. If a zoom lens can be used, it will be possible to present all the image when appropriate and to select specific parts when required. (It is remarkable how quickly the pupils' interest is engaged and imagination stirred when the image is large and close. Many original ideas are started which can be pursued into improvisation, discussion, writing, etc.)

(b)   By positioning the projector at an unusual angle to the screen it is possible to increase the effect of the images by distortion — an interesting way of using holiday slides, etc.

(c)   Project on to textures not normally used to gain additional impact (hands, brick walls, clothe, wood, clothing, etc.) Project ordinary images on to the corner of the ceiling — using the three planes of wall and ceiling. This can have bizarre effects when the image is a human or animal face.

A next step is to use one or more spot-lights in a darkened classroom. (The projectors mentioned above are suitable and there are few schools that do not possess at least one.) The spot-light should be placed on a wall at a height of 9-10 ft and, for safety, permanently secured.

A first exercise might be to throw the beam, with a wide angle, (to give maximum coverage), on the centre of the room. In large groups, or as a full class, the pupils move in and out of the light, noticing the effect on hands, faces, clothes and one another — and the shadows on the floor. This is even more interesting when the light has a primary colour filter. With two spots there is the added stimulus of coloured shadows where the beams cross.

With the room in darkness except for the spot, the shy student can lose himself in the security of the semi-darkness and experiment with strange shapes for his hands, etc. The lighting and darkened areas also encourage absorption and concentration.

A next step might be to use "strange" body shapes to suggest, in the coloured light and shadows, subjects for immediate practical work, or follow-up work in writing or painting. One way is for groups to find an unusual body position in the light, or half in it, and to hold the position absolutely still for three to four minutes. Eyes should be kept open so that the colour can continue its effect on the atmosphere, but there should be no movement of any kind — even that which comes from breathing should be kept to a minimum. The strictness of the controlled body position influences the thoughts and feelings of the pupils. (This is an excellent starting point for those classes who have done little or no creative movement work, since the very strictness of the still-ness makes them *want to move* after a time. The sense of relief helps even the most inhibited to get started. At this point the introduction of sounds or music can help consolidate the ideas and feelings and lead to characterization. If it is not possible to proceed to practical work the experiences themselves are stimuli for use in language, literature, art and music.)

The use of the spot need not be confined to lighting people but can be put to great effect with a range of filters on walls, ceilings and floors.

The suggestions given above can be enhanced and progressed by the use of moving-effects projectors. The following is only a selection of what is available:[1]

> Fleecy and Storm Clouds; Rain; Snow; Running Water; Smoke; Flames; Dissolving Colours; Liquid Wheels; Polaroid effects; Laza pulse; Liquisplode; Meteorstrobe; Rainbow-strobe; Twinkle cubes; Kaleidoscope lenses; Spectrum waves; Magic Eye; Spiral Star; Vibrating Moiré; Archimedes Spiral; Catherine Wheel; Scintillating Flower.

The above effects can be expensive but pupils can make their own moving slides from water, oil, spirit and dyes. Glass slides with plastic containers are easily obtainable from photographic shops and chemists.

The moving images can be used as stimuli for voice, speech and movement exercises, with the pupils making sounds, words, dance and gesture to accompany the changing images — all excellent exercises for sensitizing reactions and spontaneity training.

16 mm standard films can be projected for similar purposes.

[1] For full details apply to W. J. Furse & Co. Ltd, Traffic Street, Nottingham.

The images can be thrown on to the pupils themselves and when they are dressed in white the effects can be startling. All-white is not essential and ordinary shirts, blouses and PE kit are quite satisfactory. The images can also be projected on to moving cloths, polythene sheets, walls, floor and ceiling. ("A dance of flames," for example, is particularly effective if the room can be engulfed by moving images of fire and flame.)

A natural development is for the pupils not only to use these aids but to create their own. Costs of equipment are beginning to fall, and the time is near when pupils will be able to make their own radio and closed-circuit television programmes and create projects with the aid of slides and Polaroid photographs and make their own films on 8 mm, Super 8 mm and 16 mm — *as a matter of course,* and not, as is presently the case, as a special privilege. The combinations and permutations are endless and endlessly exciting but the detailed techniques of these combined arts. approaches to dramatic work are beyond the scope of this book.

2

Improvisation
(Making Responses)

The aim of this chapter is to bring the reader close to the "here-and-now" situation of some approaches to practical work. Four lessons are outlined in ways frequently experienced by the author. The lessons are typical only; they are not and cannot be models.

After the lessons and notes on pages 42—5 some general comments about method and purpose are made, and some readers may prefer to scan them first.

A LESSON WITH TEN-YEAR-OLD PUPILS:

A teacher is taking a group of 35 ten-year-old boys and girls. The place has the usual attributes of an underequipped, overcrowded old classroom. There is no blackout, special lighting, record-player, tape-recorder, slide-projector or drama blocks. The class has no previous experience of practical drama or improvisation, but has tried a number of exercises to alert the senses. In the immediate past few days they have been working on listening. The pupils are dressed in their ordinary clothes and — because there is no other space for them — are sitting at their desks. The teacher is talking.

"Outside this room there are some interesting things happening right now. We are not going to look at them — we are going to listen for them. Close your eyes and I'll tell you the first thing to listen for. Cover your eyes with your hands and rest your heads on the desk tops if you wish. All eyes closed — now! (Pause to settle). I have my eyes open and I can see a (dog — lorry — tractor — bus — girl laughing — man walking). Listen for the sound of a . . . . Listen hard. Listen."

(The exercise is repeated two or three times with a different sound.)

"Now I will close my eyes and we will all listen for a sound we think everyone else may miss. Ready!"

(After approximately 30 seconds, eyes are opened and the various sounds are described and discussed — validated if necessary or listened to by everyone. At an appropriate moment the teacher winds up the discussion and moves on.)

"After listening to the sounds of other people, we are going to concentrate on ourselves for a while. Cup your hands to your ear and mouth — bending your ear towards your mouth and making a cave so that no one can hear you and you can hear no one but yourself."

(Most pupils will know how to do this automatically — a few may need help.)

"Breathe in and out through your mouth. Breathe as slowly and as quietly as you can so that not even you can hear the sound of your breathing. Begin when you are ready."

(Time is allowed for absorption to grow and the exercise to wor This may last from 30 seconds to 5 minutes. At the first signs of interest waning the teacher continues.)

"Keep your hands in the same position and whisper a story to yourself — one that only you can hear. I shall come round and listen as closely and as carefully as I can. I shall try to hear you. Begin when you are ready."

(The teacher does as suggested and the exercise continues. Interest in it will hold for a similar length of time to the previous one. The teacher does actually try to hear and sets a standard of concentration. As long as there is no pretence it is an exciting challenge for pupils and teacher. Should it be necessary for the teacher to speak to anyone — needless to say it must be a whisper. When introducing the next exercise the teacher uses natural delivery.)

"I'm going to come round again — listening. This time you are going to talk to your neighbours — real conversations about any-thing you like — but making sure only the two of you can hear. Don't stop when I get near you — just whisper as quietly as you can. Begin when you are ready."

(The teacher checks on pairing. If convenient, because of seating arrangements, odd pupils can make groups of three. The teacher allows time for the exercise to establish and then goes on his rounds. Introducing the next activity he uses natural delivery at first.)

"Now it's my turn. Instead of me trying to hear what you have been whispering — you're going to try to hear me when I (from now on he speaks only in a whisper) WHISPER. I am going to give you some instructions and I shall know from what you do whether you hear me properly. (From this point on the teacher moves about the classroom.) All of you raise the little finger of your left hand. Girls raise the little finger of your right hand. Boys lower your fingers. All of you clench your fists high in the air. Girls lower them, still clenched, to the desks. Boys open your fists and spread your fingers," etc. . . . . .

(Explaining the next exercise the teacher resumes ordinary delivery.)

"In a moment you are to close your eyes and I am going to move about the classroom as quietly as I can. While I am very close to you you are to raise your right hand as high as possible. When I am far away you lower your right hand to the desk top. Keep your eyes closed and listen carefully."

(Dependent upon the expertise of teacher and pupils, the teacher may need to give some signals — apparent mistakes; a small cough or sigh; shoe sole scratching or squeaking on the floor; keys jangling in pocket, etc., and to close the exercise with the following from different places in the room — in a quiet whisper.)

"Listen to my voice and point to where I am."

(On the last occasion the teacher instructs the pupils to open their eyes as they point. If the last whisper is made to a wall, ceiling or cornice corner it may be possible to use the reflective acoustic qualities of the room as a deceptive factor. At an appropriate moment the teacher moves on to the next exercise.)

"Close your eyes and listen."

(The teacher scratches an empty matchbox or a nail file; the top of a table or a blackboard may be used as a substitute.)

"What does it make you think of? Don't tell me. Just think about it. Here it is again (makes sound again). What does it make you feel like? (sound again — louder). What is happening? (sound louder still) Where is it? What is it? What is it doing? (sound louder and faster) What is happening to it now? (sound slows down, quietens and ceases.) Where has it gone? What happened to it?

The pupils may be asked to respond in a number of ways to the above sequence:

(*a*)   Internally — to think and feel (not to concentrate on communication but not to inhibit necessary expression).

(*b*)   To whisper answers to the questions as and when they come to mind — eyes still closed.

(*c*)   To discuss them with partners — in whispers with eyes closed.

(*d*)   To sketch what they feel — eyes closed — in crayon or charcoal and chalk (perhaps charcoal in left hand and chalk in the right hand). A sheet of sugar paper covering the desk top.

(*e*)   To write notes — eyes closed (or open between the noises although this is not entirely conducive to absorption and continuity).

(*f*)   To write or sketch about the whole sequence when it is completed.

(*g*)   To make similar noises themselves.

(*h*)   To diagnose the actual sound source.

In the case outlined the pupils are concentrating on the experiential aspect as it is part of a progression in their work. The sequence — with variations in rhythm, loudness and question/statement — is repeated with two more noises.

1   Fingernail(s) tapping on a tin lid flat on a table or a hand mirror. A pattern might be: one nail slowly; gets faster; two nails faster; four nails very fast; side of thumb with four nails to conclude in climax.

2   Whispered sssss to ssssshhhhh — with variations made by moving lips — themselves or moved by fingers.

When appropriate the teacher moves on to the next stage.

"When you hear the next sound — make one of your hands into the thing or person, animal, human or machine that the sound suggests. It can be anything you imagine — anything you want it to be. Close your eyes and listen to the sound first — then let your hand — only one — grow into that shape. Close your eyes and listen."

(The teacher makes a series of staccato sounds — clicking in the throat; cork popping with tongue and lips; xks — xks or tch — tch or equivalent — building up the volume to aid the hand shaping and then letting it die away.)

"Keep your eyes closed — here is a different sound for the other hand."

(The teacher makes a continuant sound — rubbing the palms of the hands together; crinkling cellophane paper; rustling silk; scratching clothing — building up and dying away as before. The staccato and continuant can of course be varied according to taste and ability. The vocal could be continuant — vowels; humming; whistling; sssshhhhing or zzzhhhing; and the hand used for tapping; finger-clicking; clapping. It must be possible to perform the two together in the next stage.)

"Still keep your eyes closed. Here come both sounds — so both hands will be working together. Let your hand people, animals or things meet one another. Let them do what the noises tell them."

(The teacher starts one sound quietly and slowly — alternates the other with it. When absorption and action are established, both sounds are made together — varying in ascendancy so that conflicts may come and go. During one active conflict — while action and absorption are still at a high level — teacher abruptly stops both noises and speaks.)

"And freeze. Hold your hands absolutely still. Don't let them move. Open your eyes and look at your hands."

(The showing and sharing of hands may lead to lively conversation. If so, it should not be stopped — the next exercise should wait until the explosion of talk has peaked. If not, it should be encouraged but not forced since it is an important link between private imagination and interpersonal communication.)

"Now close your eyes again. Make your hands into the things they were. Shape them now and hold them still and motionless in front of you. We are going to do that again. But this time you are to make the noises. Similar noises if you wish — or quite different. You choose. In a moment noises and hands are going to burst into life. Ready and still. Begin . . . now."

(The "now" should be short, sharp and commanding — itself energizing the pupils to start. Their work may be slow to begin, hesitant and tentative. Teachers will decide whether it is more appropriate to stop and try for a more dynamic beginning or to let the activity grow at its own speed. The level of effort and purpose in the group will be the deciding factor. Faulty starts from accidents of hesitancy are best corrected by fresh starts; a slow growth reflecting lack of experience or expertise is best left alone. Before the interest wanes the teacher intervenes.)

"And now open your eyes. This time — watch your hand creatures as they meet one another. Watch them and listen as they speak to one another. They will have their own language — and it may be English. Now they are going to meet and talk. Begin when you are ready."

(The activity continues — when appropriate the teacher speaks again.)

"Turn to your neighbour and number yourselves one and two. Do that now. (Pause — the teacher checks on the pairing. Any pupil left over can be an additional one or two in a group of three.) Number Ones — you are going to make the sounds and noises for your partners' hands to become things and people. First a sound for one hand — then a contrasting, quite different sound for the other hand. Then both sounds together — so that the hand creatures can meet one another. By yourself decide on your first sound — but don't let your partner hear it. (Pause while they do this.) Now decide on your second sound — don't let your partner hear. (Pause) Now, Number Twos; close your eyes and get ready to make your hands into whatever you hear from your partner. First one hand; then the other; then both together. Close your eyes now. Quiet and still. Number ones — begin when you are ready."

(The activity continues. After a time the teacher brings it to a close and the partners change roles. When this has become fully established the next stage is progressed.)

"Still working with your partner — show your hand creatures. All four are going to meet and talk to one another — they will use their own language and you will make all the sounds. Get your hand creatures in good starting positions — quiet and still ready to begin. (Pause) Off you go — now."

(The activity continues for as long as fruitful — it is likely to be active and noisy.)

"Now we'll try that another way. The people on the left-hand side of the room — that's all this group — are going to make the sounds and the rest are going to close their eyes and make hand creatures. Now, sound group, those in front are going to make short, sharp, staccato sounds, and those at the back — long, drawn-out, continuing noises. We're not going to practise at all. So just think about the sounds you are going to make. Hand creatures group — you're going to use both hands together straight away. There will be plenty of different sounds for you to choose from — pick out those that interest you most and bring them to life straight away. Close your eyes and have your hands ready and still. Close your eyes now — ready and still. Sound group — ready. Begin . . . now."

(The activity continues and at an appropriate moment the teacher intervenes. The groups change over and the exercise is repeated. The teacher then draws the lesson to a conclusion.)

"We have spent a long time listening, making sounds and sometimes not making any sound at all. It's time for you to go and I'm going to sit at this table with my eyes closed. I shall keep them closed until I hear the slightest sound. You are going to leave the room in absolute silence and I shall keep my eyes closed *unless I hear a sound. The last one out can surprise me in any way — if my eyes are still closed. Remember — absolute silence. My eyes are closed now and you can begin to leave.*"

(The progress and purpose of the class will guide the teacher in deciding how many sounds to ignore. The lesson has taken approximately 45 minutes.)

That is how one teacher might tackle an introductory lesson with a group of young pupils. Here are three more examples typical of approaches with different age ranges.

A LESSON WITH TWELVE-YEAR-OLD PUPILS

The group consists of 30 twelve-year-old boys and girls. They are dressed in ordinary school clothes and may have removed ties, jackets, blazers, etc. They are in a hall that affords plenty of space and some rostrums or drama blocks. There is no blackout, lighting, tape-recorder or record-player. The teacher uses a drum, gong (a

cymbal can substitute but a gong is the better choice) and piano.
The group has had a term's previous experience. The emphasis is
on partner work.

Introduction. The class play the "spacing-out-density" game in
which they move quickly to a place where they are as far away as
possible from everybody and everything — including walls and
excluding floor, ceiling and teacher. They change positions two or
three times. (In the early stages there is often much windmill-
waving of arms. It does not assist the exercise as such, but helps
the pupils feel comfortable and does no harm.)

Relaxation. The pupils lie on the floor and the teacher talks them
through three to four minutes' relaxation — combining imaginative
situations (floating on a cloud; lying in a warm bath/shower; bones
turning to water; blood turning to mercury) with technical instructions (tense the muscles in the face; pull/push up to the ceiling;
relax fingers and toes).

Limbering. The teacher makes a number of contrasting sounds with
the drum, gong and piano and the pupils are free to move in any
way they wish. The only direction is that they *shall* move to the
sounds. (The teacher combines sharp beats on drum; reverberating
rolls on gong; low, rumbling, chords and single, repeated high notes
on piano — there is no need for knowledge of keyboard technique.

The pupils choose some of the movements and repeat them —
making their own sound accompaniment — singing, whistling,
clapping, stamping, using words and/or abstract vocalization.

Partner work

(a)   The pupils choose a partner for movement work. (They
       can be numbered One and Two and any odd pupil can be
       an extra One or Two.) They devise a movement sequence
       to the following stimuli:
            1 — move to the sound of the drum.
            2 — move to the sound of the piano.
            1 & 2 — move together to the sound of the gong (or
            when drum and piano are played together).
       The emotional overtones of the movement exercise
       can be suggested by the teacher and/or left to the pupils.
       The suggestions can be abstract (a battle of wills — con-

flict — hide-and-seek — the wind — struggle — a battle-
field) or specific (the car salesman — boxers — spider and
fly — wrestlers — cat and mouse — catching a trout).

(b) With the same partner — or a new one if the pupils wish
— Number One bodily arranges Number Two as a statue.
They change over and the exercise is repeated once or
twice. The subject of the statue can be suggested by the
teacher and/or left to the pupils. Suggestions can be
abstract or specific: (victory — defeat — flight — anger —
sorrow — fear — fort — pity — mountains — birds —
animals — air — water — earth — fire — the elements —
soldier — swimmer — sculptor — Titan — angel — coal
miner — orator — trapeze artist — juggler).

Then Number One arranges Number Two as a statue
of his own choice. He controls it and makes it move and
speak. The method of control at this stage can be left to
the pupils. When the activity is established Number One
walks behind Number Two whispering instructions so that
only Number Two can hear. A time is allowed for private
practice in pairs and then Number One directs his "living
doll" to meet and talk to the others — Number One still
being the controlling factor.

Partners change over and Number Two arranges
Number One as a statue of his own choice. Once arranged,
Number One moves — self-directed — and Number Two
creates a speaking voice for the statue and whatever
happens to it. He takes his cue from Number One's actions.
The initiative is then taken by the voice of Number Two
— still in character — and Number One interprets into
movement what he hears. After sufficient practice with
each taking the lead, the pairs work together sharing the
initiative as conditions and events require. After a time
of private practice they meet others.

Termination. Towards the close of the lesson the teacher converts
the partner work to a relaxation exercise in pairs, in which each is
the sun for the other's ice — partners' movements matching and
reflecting one another, controlling and being controlled by one
another.

After a period of relaxation one partner closes eyes and the
other directs him, by whispering, to the door of the hall — collecting clothes and dressing *en route* if necessary.

A LESSON WITH FIFTEEN-YEAR-OLD PUPILS

The group consists of 30 fifteen-year-old students — boys and girls.
They are dressed in informal appropriate clothing — jeans, slacks,
sweaters — and are in a well-equipped drama studio/workshop/
hall with blackout; flexible lighting; drapes; blocks; music and
sound equipment. (Some of this can be improvised. Classrooms
can be dimmed by drapes at the window; simple lights can be
fashioned from tin cans and junk-shop reflectors; and chairs, desks,
tables and stools can be temporary rostrum block substitutes.)

The class has a background of experience and the emphasis is
on group work.

The group is welcomed into the studio and the teacher (with
this age-group more a leader/catalyst than a teacher) suggests a
short period of self-directed relaxation. Once relaxation is
established and the atmosphere is quiet and still the leader gently
introduces music for free dance. He informs the group that they
are to use the music as they wish — in their own time.

The free dance grows and when all the group is involved the
music is abruptly silenced — but the dance continues. At intervals
the music returns and the free dance reorientates — checking time-
beat, rhythm and flow. After a number of these interruptions
(which test concentration, listening and body memory) the music
is faded out and the group continues free dance, making its own
music. At a signal from the leader the group-made music ceases and
the free dance continues in silence. Particular care is taken to make
no noise with shoes on the floor. The free dance slows down and,
as imperceptibly as possible, leads to stillness.

The leader suggests everyone should meet everyone else —
speaking to and touching everyone at least once.

At a signal from the leader the group stands still and the
students mentally note the position of the others. Eyes are closed
and contact is made — the students "passing on" one another as
they meet. They aim to meet everyone in the group in a three-to
four-minute period.

The leader directs them to bring one another to the centre of the studio. They come together in a close group and hum and sway in unison.

After a signal, the group agree — in their own time — on three to four students who shall totally relax and be carried by the rest (in groups of six or seven). No speech is permitted. The aim of the exercise is to train group sensitivity in the election/selection of students; help them relax; and to create trust.

When the exercise is completed there is open discussion regarding how well (or otherwise) it worked.

The class divides into self-selected groups of five or six. Each group will have its own space with its own spot-light and one rostrum block. (Choice of colour filters; angle of lantern; position of rostrum blocks; etc., will be the choice of each group. The previous exercises may or may not have used blackout. From this point on it is needed.)

The leader outlines the situation for the next exercise — a group improvisation — and the additional stimuli that will be fed into it. *Situation.* In each group three members know one another and the rest are strangers. At some point one of the strangers begins to weep *for no apparent reason.* There are two challenges:

(*a*) To discover the reason for the weeping.

(*b*) To remedy it.

All details of place, character, time, etc., will be left to each group to decide.

Stimuli

(*a*) The lighting will be controlled by the leader and its intensity will suggest/reflect emotional temperature according to the needs of each group.

(*b*) Sounds will be heard from time to time. They are all deemed to be near each group. They may or may not have a rational explanation and may require action from the group. In each case they will directly affect the weeping person.

(Groups are not told the nature of the sounds that will be used. The following, in the order given, is typical: thunder; marching feet; long drum roll; rain; metronome.

The groups are given only sufficient and necessary time to

prepare essentials — to set blocks, lights, drapes and agree
basics regarding place, time and character. It is best if no agree-
ment is made about who shall weep, or where and when. This
should be left to arise spontaneously during the group work.

The leader checks that groups and ingredients are ready and
gives a signal to begin. The lights and sound will be introduced
when *needed* by one or more groups — plenty of time being
allowed for the improvisation to progress before any one of them
is used.

A THEMATIC LESSON : "ODYSSEUS — OR TALES OF THE SICILIAN SEA"

The class conditions are similar to those in the lesson with twelve-
year-old pupils given earlier. The emphasis is on the development
of thematic work from individual exercises to full class involvement in a united effort.

The following story outline is given in a style that is suitable
for delivery over music at first and, in the later stages, in conjunction with a drum and gong. It would not be used in the
actual lesson until the preparatory exercises had been completed.
The story outline is given here so that the exercises may be seen
in their proper context.

"Odysseus, King of Ithaca, was known for his wisdom, his
courage, his eloquence and his cunning. One of his more famous
schemes was the Wooden Horse of Troy.

"During his many adventures he heard about the Sirens. What
he heard so fascinated him that he became impatient to come
face to face with the incredible creatures.

"The Sirens lived on an island not far from the Straits of
Messina. They had many shapes and many names. Some were red-
plumed birds with young girls' faces. Some were half women and
half sea birds, and some were half women and half fish. Some were
demons, some were monsters and some were nymphs. Three of the
best-known Sirens were called Parthenope, Ligea and Leucosia.
They were all dangerous and they all made beautiful music.

"There was a catch, of course. Their singing was so attractive
that anyone who heard it forgot everything — listening even till
they died of hunger.

"The Sirens were proud of the magic of their voices. Proud enough to jump from their rocks whenever they failed to lure a victim to his death. They were well known for their passionate and fatal attraction for sailors.

"Odysseus was one of the few sailors to see the Sirens, hear their singing and not to be lured to a watery grave. The enchantress Circe advised him, when his boat approached Siren Island, to have himself lashed to the mast and the ears of his crew plugged with beeswax.

"Thus he was able to listen and watch, yet still live to tell his fantastic story.

"Odysseus also managed to avoid the other dangers in the Straits of Messina — the twin terrors of the rock Scylla and the whirlpool Charybdis.

"Charybdis — daughter of old man Neptune and Mother Earth herself — lived under an enormous fig-tree. She was a terrifying monster who lived on sea-water. Three times each day would she gobble the seas and three time would she throw them up again. Her gorging made a whirlpool so powerful that no ship caught in it stood a chance of steering clear. Many sailors, avoiding the whirlpool Charybdis, floundered on the rocks of Scylla.

"Scylla at one time had been a beautiful young woman but had been changed by a spell into a many-headed, dog monster. She was so terrified that she threw herself into the Straits of Messina. Circe straightway changed her into rocks to put her out of her misery. During storms in the Straits of Messina, sailors say a yelping roar can be heard — as if from the mouths of hideous puppies.

(The teacher fades out music and takes up drum and gong.)

"You are now Scylla (the teacher plays drum) or Charybdis (the teacher plays gong). Choose which you are and get into your beginning positions. The drum is for Scylla and the gong for Charybdis. Move when you hear your sound. Ready and still."

Before the material is presented in this story/music form, there will have been these introductory exercises:

Relaxation. The teacher talks the pupils through situations in which they are carried — swimming or floating — by the surf, waves and swell of the sea. (A gong music or sound effects can

be used if needed.) This can lead easily into the next exercise.
Free dance limbering. The exercise begins with water dripping,
grows into a trickle of water, then into a stream, a river, a sea
and into the wild ocean. Finally it subsides into a quiet inland
sea or lake. (Suitable music would be useful support/stimulus.)
Vocal limbering. The spirits of this last-mentioned inland sea (lake)
begin to murmur — whispering and wailing like ghosts of snakes.
(Music can be used to support the pupils beginning sounds and
faded out once these are established.)
Individual work. As the music and/or sound dies away the teacher
talks the class through an individual, imaginative sequence:

In a jungle in South America — marshes — swamps — sinking
sands — whirlpools and rocks. Ever-present is the will-o'-the-wisp.
An expedition is searching for uranium (or equivalent — anything
precious for which listening devices can be used). All round are
the noises of the jungle. They must not be allowed to deter or
obtrude — neither must the thoughts, feelings and sensations that
stem from physical exhaustion (faces in the bushes — trees
appearing to be strange monsters — and other hallucinatory
features). The search continues until darkness falls quickly.
Exhausted, everyone rests.

Rest Period

This exercise forms a natural break between the physical exertion
of the previous work and the concentrated session that is to
follow. After a few moments of relaxation, the teacher quietly
starts the music that will lead into the next stage. (Suitable music
here is a "A Whiter Shade of Pale," "Sound of a Bass," "Meditation"
"Gesang der Jünglingen." If no record-player is available, drums,
gongs and piano/guitar with paper between the strings can create
suitable sounds. Feed-back from an amplifier and/or tape-recorder,
re-recorded and played back at half or quarter speed can provide
appropriate accompaniment/backing.) Over the music, the teacher
tells the story — perhaps as suggested in the story outline given
earlier. From this point onwards, the development of the lesson
should be unbroken. The first stage is growth into individual
creative work as suggested at the end of the story outline.

Individual

The pupils respond individually as Scylla when the drum is played and Charybdis when the gong is played. The teacher will vary the signals as much as possible to stimulate contrast within the disciplines of "rock" and "whirlpool" movements. It is likely that the pupils will most readily respond in terms of silent dramatic dance to the stimuli, but there is no reason why they should not vocalize at this stage, if they wish.

Pairs

(a) The pupils work with partners. Number One being Scylla and Number Two being Charybdis. With the stimuli of drum and gong still being played by the teacher, the pupils practise and change roles. They work in unison and also in opposition.

(b) Using the music from the opening sequence of the story outline (now used without words from the teacher) Number One becomes Odysseus and Number Two one of the sirens. Number One tries to retain concentration on listening or looking at anything real in the space and Number Two, using and working with the music, tries to break this concentration and "lure" Number One away from the object of his attention. The pupils practise and change roles.

Fours

In each group of four there is one Odysseus, one Siren, one Scylla and one Charybdis. Odysseus meets the other three separately and/ or together. The teacher stimulates their dance/drama-movement conflict with drum, gong and music. It may be useful to arrange for a sound device to support Odysseus at this stage and piano or guitar would be suitable as would any wind instrument — including recorder and penny whistle. Alternatively, each member of the group of four may wish to make their own sounds, be they with instruments, abstract vocalization or exact verbalization.

Eights

The method as outlined for groups of four is repeated. The grouping might be as follows:

	Odysseus	Scylla	Charybdis	Sirens
	1	2	2	3
or	2 (1 crew)	2	2	2
or	5 (4 crew)	1	1	1

Full Class

After the preparatory practice and exploratory improvisation in
pairs, fours and eights, the class should be ready to see the
practical work through to a finished co-operative event. By this
time it might last from three to fifteen minutes and the teacher
might still be providing the external sound stimuli or the pupils
might have taken it all over for themselves. The piece might
have moved towards a speech-orientated event. The progress
from individual ideas through pair work, etc., to organized formalized class participation involves much horizontal development,
co-operation and some discussion. How the groups are consti-
tuted and how many will have leaders of their own will depend
upon inter-personal relationships within the class. Groupings
might be as follows:

	Odysseus	Scylla	Charybdis	Sirens
	1	10	10	11
or	8	8	8	8
or	20	4	4	4

How many in each group are actual "Odysseus" and how many
members of the crew is a matter for local discussion between
teacher and pupils. So is the question as to whether or not each
Scylla, Charybdis and Siren group have a leader — perhaps with
special powers. The details of the story-line chosen by the class
will dictate the answers to these and many questions.

IMPROVISATION: what it is and how it works

The patterns of class work described above are only some of the
many approaches to improvised work which, in essence, is a
matter of the pupils' personal responses to the external stimuli
presented by the teacher. These personal, subjective responses
may be made in the solo, private situation of class work (when
everyone is deeply absorbed in individual expression); in pair

and small group work; or in large group/full class work. The
pattern is likely to be:

Personal   —   the stimuli mainly external to the individual.

Partner   —   the stimuli external and internal to the pair.

Group   —   the stimuli mainly internal to the group.

There is two-way movement in all three sections. Incident can
lead to the creation of atmosphere (external) or atmosphere can
lead to the creation of incident (internal).

Improvisation can be divided into three main stages:

1 *Creation* (Beginning).

Action and reaction — injection. (Sometimes there will be spontaneous combustion. Sometimes compression and ignition will be
needed to create the creative explosion.)

It is a period of vertical absorption: activity will be spontaneous
— emotive, imaginative and kinetic. In spite of insecurity and in-
stability (the work is creative) it will be typified by the immediacy
and fullness of the explosive responses.

2 *Organization* (Middle).

Analysis and synthesis — digestion

It is a period of vertical absorption and horizontal concentration: activity will be mainly intuitive — imaginative variation and
manipulation with intellectual and rational exploration and investi-
gation. Hesitancy and enthusiasm; doubt and confidence; anxiety
and inspiration will go hand in hand. An important feature will be
thoughtful discussion.

3 *Execution* (End).

Termination and fruition — exhaustion.

It is a period of horizontal concentration: activity will be
marked by its intellectual control. It will be formalized, sure and
unfaltering. There will be a sense of confidence, excellence and
joy in purpose and action. An essential element will be the re-
creation of the symbolic ritual — valid as long as it carries a charge
that is corporate and relevant.

Purpose and Value

Only a genius carries within himself sufficient and necessary
stimuli for creative growth and artistic achievement. Improvisation
feeds in the stimuli and encourages the responses. It prepares the

person to be alert and so enables chance to enter a prepared mind. This element of "chance" or "the found" is important in improvisation. *Creation* most frequently comes about by *accident* and the finished art is almost always achieved by *design.*

Improvisation is not a training for facile ad-libbing — compensation for lack of care or commitment. It is not an easy make-do-and mend method nor is it boring repetitions of the trivia of living. (Now be a tree. Now be another tree. Now be a bush!)

Improvisation is more of a severe apprenticeship, concerning itself with matters of moment. It poses questions to which there is no abiding answer. It creates situations which challenge cliché responses. It throws the individual pupil back on his own resources — reminding him constantly of the transience and unlikeliness of things. It helps put him into direct touch with the experience of change and the insecurity of the human condition. It helps him become confident in his knowledge of that insecurity and enables him more easily to accommodate change and growth. It does not set out to help him learn how things were or how they are so much as how they might become.

It helps to practise innovation; live with change and cope with being taken off guard — personally and socially.

Improvisation highlights the problems of creating order out of chaos and achieving the rational in the midst of the irrational. Chaos, disorder and the irrational work strongly in our subconscious. Improvisation helps tap the subconscious, keep in touch with thoughts and feelings and achieve spontaneity and flexibility in responses. It creates a temporary factitious security in a known environment with a trusted leader and this offers a release from the shackles of prosaic actuality so that flights of imagination can expose and explore poetic reality. The world of the spirit is experienced, expressed and communicated. It is breathed in and lived out.

Improvisation exposes the novel; the hidden; the unexpected. It takes pupils through a comprehensive exploration of the possible in any given experience — by-passing the probable and glimpsing the impossible: those perfections and excellencies that are the targets of human aspiration at its best.

The most *dramatic "impossibilities"* for good and evil co-exist in the human spirit. Improvisation shows the secret places of the soul and these white, red and black "impossible" forces. The stupid man gives thoughtless vent to them all. The crafty man disguises them. The wise man accepts them — inspects, selects and controls.

Thus improvisation — generally and specifically — prepares pupils for possible life situations and offers a theatre arts training at the same time. Above all it helps pupils accommodate insecurity and change; accept innovation and growth; and, perhaps most importantly, increase self-awareness.

The Role of the Teacher.
The most important role of the teacher is that of a selector and controller of stimuli and trigger-starters. His personal involvement and commitment will help the group feel at ease and encourage its creativity. His involvement may progress to physical participation. (This, however, can bring with it complex problems — only one of which is that absorption with one group can deny full and proper oversight to the rest.)

There is no place for a cosy approach to dramatic improvisation. If pupils are to bite on human experience the teacher must be the final, resilient *thing* that offers appropriate strength and resistance. This may mean a love-hate relationship with the group. Certainly, from time to time, the teacher will need to be a brick wall, pin-prick or H-bomb. He will also need to be, from time to time, a safety-net and feather-bed. He is a combination of catalyst, agent-provocateur and entrepreneur, as the following exercises, particularly the later ones, will demonstrate. They are suitable for any age range. Their selection should depend upon the development of the class, the relationship between teacher and pupils and, most importantly, whether they recommend themselves to the reader. Except in the spirit of open experiment it is wisest to try only those exercises which immediately or intuitively appeal.

EXERCISES
(Unless the improvisations stem from another activity which leads into them easily and naturally, it is good to start dramatic work with relaxation exercises.)

For Relaxing

1 *Technical*

(a) Tensing and relaxing separate parts of the body; twisting fingers and hands; pulling faces; reaching, pulling, pushing.

(b) Lying on the back and reaching with every muscle to the ceiling — pulling and holding breath until collapsing into relaxation

(These exercises can be undertaken individually with the full class working at the same time or in pairs with partners helping to check tension and relaxation. Testing for "floppy-wet-fish" hands is always enjoyable.)

2 *Imaginative*

(a) A piece of ice or a snowman slowly melting;
      sugar dissolving in tea, coffee or warm water.

(b) Lying on a cloud, a water-bed or bed of foam, or
      in a warm bath.

(c) Standing in a warm shower; and, later,
      testing the ice-cold sea.

(d) Skin made of glass;
      bones made of ice;
      blood turns to grit and sand; dust and ashes; mercury;
      warm water;

(e) Floating in outer space;
      walking on the moon (little gravity);
      walking on Venus (great gravity);
      walking on a new planet where gravity changes.

(f) Being matchstick- or pin-men; then
      fluffy woolly dolls; then
      a bubble or a feather; then
      floating in a bubble or on a feather.

For Sensitizing Responses

1 Watching bubbles burst and making noises and movements with them.

2 Playing the "Scissors-Paper-Stone" game.

3 Mirror games with partners — using parts of the body separately and together — with and without mirrors.

4 Responding to "flash-card" use of photographs, slides, sounds, words from teacher or partner. (Sharp staccato

sounds are good starters and early words should be simple. For example Big, Little, Fat, Thin, High, Low.) The responses can be physical or vocal — or both.

5 Balancing on one leg with eyes closed — individual at first; in pairs later; in small groups.

6 Jumping in the air (at least 6 in. above the ground) and landing on one or both feet — eyes closed.

(Progress can easily be made from the exercises in Chapter I. When absorption in any exercise is established the following questions can be used:

(*a*) What does it (the sensation) suggest?

(*b*) What does it mean?

(*c*) What do you feel about it?

(*d*) What might it be?

(*e*) What does it mean?

(*f*) What can you do about it?

(*g*) What would you like to do about it?

The pupils can also be told to become the sensation and bring it to life with separate parts of the body; with the whole body. A tape-recorder is particularly helpful here. Music, noises, sounds and sound effects — natural, re-recorded, edited and treated — are all excellent stimuli.

Individual Exercises (full class working at the same time)

1 The following are some broad disciplines that can obtain through the whole of one lesson. The content of the lesson is otherwise completely normal (for example crowd scenes on a beach, in a hotel at a fairground, etc.). If the disciplines are to create genuine responses they must *continue until they bite.*

(*a*) No speech of any kind.

(*b*) Vocalization only: no words.

(*c*) One word only at any one time.

(*d*) Two words only at any one time.

(*e*) Gibberish only.

(*f*) Singing only.

(*g*) Using only the left hand.

(*h*) Using only the right hand.

    (*i*)   Using only the left leg (not letting the other touch the
            ground).
    (*j*)   Using only the right leg.
    (*k*)   Keeping the left eye closed.
    (*l*)   Keeping the right eye closed.
    (*m*)   Keeping both eyes closed (or blindfolded).
    (*n*)   Using ear-plugs.

Exercises requiring Immediate Response to Stimulus

(The pupils wait prepared to receive the stimulus and immediately
respond to it.)

(*a*) *Drum beats:* speed and volume carried. They can suggest
gun shots (shooting and being hit); lightning flashes; steps up or
down a rock face or glacier; a trapeze artist taking steps, etc. (the
work can easily progress to partner work with partners clapping
hands or stamping to give the signal).

(*b*) *Gong:* single beats and rolls varied in speed and volume.
Thunder; wind; waves (rivers and sea); wading; swimming, sailing,
boating.

(*c*) *Piano:* single notes; trills; chords; glissandi. (All these can
be executed by non-experts.)

The suggestions for drums and gongs are all suitable for work
with the piano.

Exercises requiring Immediate Response to Signals

(The pupils are fully absorbed in the stimulus and at the signal
give immediate expression to their thoughts and feelings.

(*a*) Photographs, cartoons, paintings and/or slides are distributed to the pupils. They absorb themselves until lost in their
imagination. At a given signal from the teacher they bring to life
whatever they have been imagining:

    (*i*)   in movement;
    (*ii*)   vocally;
    (*iii*) together.

(The stimuli can vary from small hand-held photographs or
individual slide-viewers to large projected images on the walls,
floor or ceiling.)

(*b*) Objects found in the room are also suitable stimuli. For example marks on the floor, fire extinguishers, window catches, door knobs, pens, pencils, erasers, books, vases, shoes and lamps. All are suitable objects for absorption.

(The pupils can become the objects of their concentration, beinging them to life in any way that they wish.)

(c) The pupils tell a story round a circle. At first they use only one word at each turn, then a phrase at each turn, and later full sentences.

(d) The pupils respond to a single word repeated *many times* by the teacher in *different ways.* They respond:

  (i)   in words;
  (ii) in movement;
  (iii) by creating a character. As a later development the work can move into pairs or small groups — alternatively, the characters can meet one another in the full class situation.

(e) Each pupil has a self-chosen "treasure" (a purse, a hat, a sword, a pet rabbit, etc.) and the teacher tells a story that involves this personal treasure. The pupils respond and dramatize the events as they are described by the teacher. Here is an example of such a story:

"I am going to tell you a story. It will be about a very special object — an object of your choice, that you own : an important object; a treasure even — certainly a treasure to you. You can choose what it is to be. It might be a purse, a sword, a toy, a pet animal, a gold sovereign or a balloon. Choose your object now.

(The teacher allows time for this.)

"As I tell the story of what happens to you and your special object, you are going to bring it alive and do whatever I say in the story — when I say it. I shall call it your treasure — and you will know it is your chosen object I mean. When I get to a certain point in the story, I shall stop and leave you to finish it in your own way. Are you all ready?

(The teacher allows an opportunity for those who may not have fully understood to ask questions.)

"The story begins with you asleep in bed. It is late at night and you are asleep. Everything is quiet and still — quiet and still; until you hear a faint scratching noise at the foot of your bed. You are

still half asleep and not sure of what you heard, so you listen carefully. Yes! there it is — a faint scratching at the foot of the bed.
You get up and go to put on the light — but it does not work. You
flick the switch once or twice, but no light comes. You go to the
window and draw back the curtains. The moonlight shines into
your room and you can see quite clearly. You can see quite clearly
that your treasure is not on the chair but on the floor in the middle
of the room — and it is moving very slowly to the foot of the bed
— towards the scratching noise that has now got stronger. You
pick up your treasure, intending to put it back on the chair, but
no sooner do you have it in your hands than it is on the floor again
— like magic. You are not going to be easily defeated or put off.
You pick up your treasure again — but for the second time it is
straight away on the floor. How strange! You stand and watch it
as it begins to move slowly towards the scratching noise at the
foot of the bed. It will soon be there — it is nearly there now.
You look at the bed and just make out a slight movement at one
corner. Quietly and slowly — on tip-toe — you go to it and lift the
bedspread. And what do you find making the scratching noise and
waiting for your treasure to arrive on its visit? . . . . Well; that is up
to you . . . . Finish up the story in any way you like . . . . Now."

(*f*) Each pupil has a self-chosen character. The teacher tells
a story and the pupils dramatize what happens to their individual
character. Here is an example of such a story:

The pupils may choose characters like : a cowardly giant; a
clever little girl; a frightened old man; a speaking frog; a boastful
boy — and enact the story bending the details to fit their character

The story could go like this:

"You are on your way to the dentist. You have been preparing
yourself for a week because the dentist has said he is going to give
you a special anaesthetic so you will have pleasant dreams and not
feel a thing. You arrive at the dentist's and are ushered straight in.
You sit in the chair and rest back. The dentist's assistant gives you
the mask. You breathe in and soon you are floating gently — like
a huge balloon in a gentle wind. Floating gently until you fall
asleep and dream.

"In your dream you see two silver-haired old gentlemen rowing
a small boat on a wide lake. The surface of the water is as smooth

as glass and there is silence everywhere. The two old men stop
rowing and lift a small silver casket from the bottom of the boat.
They look at it keenly. One of them opens the lid and looks inside.
You hear him say 'They're all there. Every single one. Beauties
aren't they?' He sighs and closes the lid. 'Ah, well. What a pity.'
He gently places the casket on the surface of the water and you
are surprised to see it does not sink. The two old gentlemen do
not even look at it but row smoothly away. The silver casket floats
on the lake like a lily pad. The moonlight shines on it and it is
reflected until all you can see are shining icicles of light. You close
your eyes — the light is so bright. In a moment you open them
again. The light is still shining, but not from the moonlight. It
comes from the dentist's battery of bright, overhead lamps. He is
talking to you. 'Well done. It's all over. You can sit up now.'

"You do as the dentist suggests — still a little hazy from the
anaesthetic. You can see the dentist's tray in front of you — with
all shining instruments laid out . . . . and in the middle of the tray,
like a prize, is the silver casket."

(Teacher now continues the story or leaves the pupils to
improvise.)

(*g*) Each pupil decides upon a series of events that a character
is to undergo. The teacher then describes the character the pupils
are to use. (These last exercises give the pupils the initiative of the
original choice and require them to discipline themselves through
a series of unexpected events. Some of the pupils may believe they
become involved in impossible situations — this is where the improvisation begins to challenge and bite.)

(*h*) Teacher or pupils use a wheel-spinning device to create
quick cameos. Wheels and arrows can be made up containing details
of the following:

  (*i*)   age;
  (*ii*)   occupation;
  (*iii*) colours;
  (*iv*)   moods;
  (*v*)   times;
  (*vi*)   weather;
  (*vii*) objects.

(One or more wheels are spun and the pupils immediately respond
to the details as stated.)

General

  (a) Pupils use objects in any way that they wish *except as what
they are* (shoes, chairs, pens, jackets, hats, etc.).

  (b) The pupils are all uninvited guests at a party — none of them
wishes to be found. Similarly they are all spies at a conference.

  (c) One person (selected by the teacher) is an outsider at a
special function. The rest of the pupils try to identify the outsider.

  (d) The pupils are all guests at a party — they change characters
each time they meet a new guest.

Partner Work
(Most of the previous exercises can easily be developed or adapted
to suit pair work.)

  1 Different ways of meeting and parting.

  2 Different ways of saying hello and goodbye.

  3 Camera operator/film director working with actor/stunt man,
etc.

  4 Using masks, make-up — mirrors. Partner chooses the mask
— does the make-up — selects clothes, etc., for the other.

     Puppets — hand, stick, and life-size — can be used in a similar
way. (Partners can *become* the masks or the puppets or they can
use the mask or the puppet as an *extension role* so that when partner meets partner there are four characters involved.)

     Similarly models and collage, matchboxes and pipe-cleaner
men can also meet model to model and/or pupil to pupil. (A good
beginning for character sketches is for each pupil to create a
picture character where each feature is drawn from a different
photograph or picture. For example two separate ears and two
separate eyes.)

  5 Partners choose any kind of activity and practise it. They
then repeat the activity with one standing and one kneeling; one
sitting one lying; one standing one lying; both kneeling, etc.

  6 Work out slow-motion fight sequences with a variety of
weapons.

  7 Work out slow-motion sequences for paired activities —

chopping down a tree; riding a tandem; operating a machine; handling a heavy weight; etc.

8 Partners try to get each other to undertake some specific task — each trying not to be "caught out." (Each partner writes down the task before the exercise or alternatively teacher hands out cards with instructions on them.)

9 Partner wants the other to go or to stay. Partner's task is to attempt the opposite.

10 Working in pairs — being hunted and hunting. Being hunted together; hunting together; one hunting, the other being hunted. Can be repeated in slow motion. (An exercise which exposes this device: partners watch one another eagle-eyed — both trying to change position *unnoticed in full view of the other*.)

11 Door-to-door salesman; car salesman; visit to doctor; employer meeting with employee — one being interviewed for a job, two being made redundant. (The meetings can also be arranged in two circles — the inner circle moving round one place each time.)

12 Question-and-answer technique:

(*a*) sounds;
(*b*) movements;
(*c*) sounds and movements together;
(*d*) words.

(The aim is to achieve a sympathy of rhythm. Number One asks the question — or makes the statement and Number Two finds an appropriate answer or response. In the early stages it is simplest if the response is in the same medium as the initial statement. The exercise can also be worked to a metronome or teacher's control from the drum.)

13 Movement, speech and full character improvisations based on opposites:

Heat and cold	water and stone	high and low
fire and water	quick and slow	crude and sophisticated
sun and snow	moving and still	rich and poor
north pole and equator		

valleys of the sun   mountains of the moon

under the ocean and in the air

truth and lies	Daedalus and Icarus
young and old	Tortoise and Hare
ugly and beautiful	Othello and Iago
clever and stupid	Cain and Abel
Gods and Devils	Punch and Judy
Mouse and elephant	Peacock and Crow
Methuselah and Peter Pan	Samson and Delilah
Adam and Eve	Steptoe and Son
Doctor Who and a Dalek	Dr Jekyll and Mr Hyde
Soldier and Pacifist	Speaker and Heckler
Fascist and Communist	Robot and Ghost

(If more variations are wanted for partner work on opposites the following can be added stimuli or control factors: a) restricted space on the floor b) on a chair c) partners always touching one another d) partners never touching one another e) absolute silence; etc.)

Group Improvisations
(Most individual and partner work can be progressed easily to group work. 6-8 is a good number for a general group.)

1   A secret society (revolutionaries or equivalent) one member of which is a traitor. (The member can be nominated by the teacher for the exercise or not.)

2   On a life-raft — a thousand miles to go — there are two too many for survival.

3   In the group all are machines except one who is a human.

4   In the group all are humans except one who is a machine.

5   A pop group (or sports team or equivalent) an essential member of which wishes to leave.

6   A group meets — one member arrives much later than the others and "something" has been set up for his arrival.

7   In the group a metronome is hidden — one member is blind-folded and has to find it while others try to distract him. (This exercise is typical of those that can be used at many levels: sensory reception and perception; group sensitivity; concentration and imaginative stimulus.)

8   Some groups work well with a title and others find it a hindrance and reduce its essence to trivia. Care should be taken in

its introduction. Any of the titles from the partner work list of opposites can be used. The following are typical:
Waiting; Wanting; Patience; Intolerance; A Birth; A Death; Loving; Hating; Hope; Despair.

9   Some groups work well with the description of an event. This also can be problematical: some fall into the trap of busy, organized activity involving nothing dramatic.

Typical suggestions are:
A mine disaster; Highjack in the air or at sea; A forced landing; Discovery in the tomb; Lost in the jungle; No water in the desert.

Or crowd scenes:
Supermarket; Crowded beach; Airport; Busy hotel; Youth club; Football crowd; The Frozen Thames and the Fire of London; Ghouls at a road or air crash.

Developments

Once an improvisation has been started the following can be injected into it to keep the improvisatory element strong or to give the work a new direction. (N.B. The pupils should be given clear directions that every event or incident is part of their improvisation unless there is a clearly agreed signal from the teacher to stop.)

Events to be injected

1   The music stops.
2   The smell of gas.
3   The lights go out.
4   A total electricity failure.
5   Earthquake — landslide — flood.
6   Car accident nearby.
7   The doors are locked from the outside.
8   One member of the group starts to laugh.
9   One member of the group starts to cry.
10 All members of the group are struck dumb.
11 One member of the group is struck dumb.
12 All members of the group are struck blind.
13 One member of the group is struck blind.
14 Telephone rings — knock at the door — telegram arrives.
15 A mysterious sound begins (tapping, knocking, squeaking,

drilling, ticking, dripping, rattling of chain); the sound continues
for as long as it is useful.

16 A scream is heard.

17 Or one member of the group screams.

18 One member of the group is poisoned.

19 One member of the group faints.

20 Some of the chairs are taken away.

21 All the chairs are taken away.

22 All essential properties are taken away.

23 Strange objects appear (for example a brown paper parcel,
a hat or shoe, a large brick, a tumbler).

(Even in an ordinary classroom putting the lights on or off;
opening curtains; slamming the door; etc., can work effectively
provided the pupils know that they are signals to be incorporated
into the improvisations.)

Endings

It is best to plan the work so that improvisations burn out in time
for the pupils to have a short period of relaxation before leaving.
They may be going to a contrasting ethos and environment — in
any case it will be different and they should be allowed time to
reorientate.

If, for one reason or another, improvisations are running over
time they can be ended by:

      (a) the teacher entering into the improvisation in a suitable
           role;

      (b) the teacher injecting a terminating event into the
           improvisation;

      (c) the teacher using a warning signal (not too obtrusively)
           two to three minutes before it is actually time to stop.

The more smoothly improvisations can conclude the better it is
for all concerned. It is important that the pupils themselves should
learn to control the element of time. They will not always be
protected by someone with a warning bell.

3

Movement and Speech
(Practising Skills)

With senses alert and experiences mobilized the pupil needs opportunities to practise the skills which increase his flow of expression and improve the possibility of communication. The skills are divided into two main areas:

MOVEMENT/GESTURE — When formalized, refined and charged: Dance.

LANGUAGE — When formalized, refined and charged: Poetry.

When the two areas come together they provide the tools of experience and communication. When they are formalized, refined and charged they become Theatre.

Basically, we move and speak in order to survive as individuals; tribes; nations and species. A special feature of man's struggle for survival, growth and fulfilment is his urge to communicate person-to-person.

INTER-PERSONAL RELATIONSHIPS

Movement, gesture and speech are motivated, inspired and stimulated best by charged inter-personal relationships — sometimes forced into flow; sometimes easily free-wheeling.

Inter-personal relationships, in brief and over-simplified, consist of image *building* or image *reducing* ("ego-boost" or "status destruction").

"A" can build or reduce the image of "B" as follows, shown in diagram form:

+ = Active Building   − = Active Reducing   . = Passive Role

$A+$	$B.$	Extension of A: Praise, virtue
$A-$	$B.$	Negation of A: Blame, guilt
$A+$	$B-$	Extension of A and negation of B

57

$A-$	$B+$	Negation of A and extension of B
$A+$	$B+$	Mutual Admiration
$A-$	$B-$	Self-defeating relationship.

(These are all with A taking an active role. There is also $A . B-$ and $A . B+$.)

In the drama lesson two conditions are needed:

1   $A - B$ inter-personal relationships exposed, flexible and charged enough to promote the need to communicate person-to-person.

2   The stimuli must be appropriate
   (a)   for movement — things movement can best express;
   (b)   for language — things language can best express.

Movement and gesture best express the primitive, instinctive and emotional.

Language best expresses the rational, subtle and civilized.

On most occasions a delicate blend is needed but, from time to time, movement or language will need to be specially emphasized. In the class situation it is not difficult to plan for this emphasis and to use suitable stimuli. For a chapter concerning itself with practising skills it is not unreasonable for the practical element to be stressed. The rest of this chapter deals, therefore, with the physical realization of these ideas and is given over to practical exercises.

EXERCISES

The following exercises are grouped under the main heads of Movement and Language. They can be used separately or together in almost any combination and in many different ways.

Basic Variables for any lesson

The following variables will transform or modify the exercises according to need. The disciplines can be introduced, almost without exception, into all the exercises and used by full classes for individual work; with partners; in small groups.

A

1   In the classroom; hall; studio/workshop; stage.
2   In the open air.
3   At home and in the street.
4   At desks; gathered round tables; standing by desks.

5 With drama blocks; desks; chairs — or with no opportunity of changing level.

B

1 Place (for example, seashore; hilltop; prison; palace; bus; hotel).
2 Attitude (for example, anger; pleasure; hate; anxiety).
3 Occupation.
4 Age.
5 Period (Past; Present; Future).

C

1 Body noise permitted (the sound of body movements; clock; clothing; shoes on floor; etc.)
2 No noise permitted.
3 With metronome; beat music; atmospheric and/or sound effects.
4 With hand mirrors — with full-length mirrors.
5 Actions performed at double speed or half speed.
6 Stress horizontal work (In — Out) or vertical (Up — Down).
7 "Jump" starts or slow growth.
8 "Freeze" techniques in the full flow of each exercise.

D

1 Writing (and/or painting, sketching, etc.) before, during or after any exercise.
2 For movement exercises — each pupil speaks aloud a full description of what he is doing — *while it is happening.*
3 For speech exercises — partner describes what is happening — *while it is happening.*

Movement Exercises

1 Growing into people, animals, creatures, things and abstract shapes taken from:

> real life;
> photographs;
> sketches and cartoons;
> films and moving cartoons (include television);
> slides and filmstrips.

> The pupils can use the exercises to create
> (*a*) still body shapes;
> (*b*) moving body shapes;

and the exercises can be undertaken:
    while looking at visuals;
    from memory.
(Films and television programmes are particularly stimulating
for these exercises, when the sound is turned down.)
    2 Copying people's movements (taken from real life or film or
photograph) using separate parts of the body only — head, hand,
ankle, shoulder, elbow, etc.
    Using whole body shapes and total movement patterns
(walking, sitting, standing, cycling, occupational movements, etc.)
    This can be undertaken particularly effectively as mirror work.
    3 The pupils sit, stand, lie, fall, kneel, etc., in as many different
and contrasting ways as possible. The differences and contrasts can
be used easily for individual work — they are also particularly
challenging for partner and group work.
    4 Representing the shapes of:
    objects found in the room;
    puppets operated by partners;
    things brought to school: sweets (liquorice allsorts and Quality
        Street are good shapes), toys, sculpture, jumping beans, and
        even pet mice, hamsters and cats if they can be suitably con-
        trolled.
    5 Making body shapes for individual sounds and words in:
        (a) still shapes;
        (b) moving shapes.
    The sounds can be made by the pupils as they move; by
partners for them; by the teacher or from tape.
    6 Making body shapes for machines. (Heavy machinery — light
machinery — electric — steam — clockwork — etc.)
    (The shapes can be still and/or moving and the noises can be
made as in Exercise 5 above.)
    7 The pupils are given details of a character, emotion or occu-
pation. The details are described aloud by the teacher, duplicated
and distributed or written on a board. The pupils create movements and gestures to reflect the descriptions:
        (a) specific movements in isolation;
        (b) specific movements are grouped together — by indivi-
            duals, in pairs or in groups;

(*c*) the movements are put together to create a unified whole.

8 The pupils represent characters, creatures and things from descriptions supplied by the teacher:

(*a*) one single isolated movement or gesture to be repeated continuously;

(*b*) two isolated movements or gestures to be repeated;

(*c*) a selection of movements and gestures to be repeated.

(A continuation for this exercise is to grow into sound work, vocalization and speech.)

9 The pupils wear "funny" clothes and create still and moving body shapes to reflect the feeling of the clothes.

The pupils wear ordinary clothes in an extraordinary way and create still and moving body shapes to reflect the feelings.

10 Conducting music; being a metronome; painting a huge picture of the music in the air; painting a picture of words in the air. The movements are extended from painting a picture in the air to dancing it over a space and adding sounds and words.

11 Using hoops, balls, ropes, etc., for real games — the pupils then repeat the games without the aids.

12 Use climbing apparatus (boxes, ropes, bars, and any other gymnastic equipment) for real games and activities. The pupils then repeat the movements without the aids.

13 Handling objects (suitcase, chair, teapot, piano, etc.), then repeating the movements without the objects.

14 The pupils create body shapes (still and moving) that are the same as everyone else in the class. The exercise might be undertaken first with a leader and later without a leader. (This last method is difficult and complex but extremely enjoyable and rewarding.)

15 In the classroom or in the playground the pupils play hide-and-seek *in slow motion.*

16 The pupils make still photographs of faces and hands. After a little practice they make many of them, one immediately after another, and all *to be different.*

17 The pupils "speak" using only their hands, feet, shoulders, elbows, eyes, eyebrows, etc.

18 Any kind of mirror game:

(a) at first with a partner and in slow motion;
(b) with a partner in double quick time;
(c) in groups in slow motion;
(d) in groups in ordinary time;
(e) in groups in double quick time;

19 This exercise can be undertaken by the full class but is best introduced in groups of six to eight.

The pupils sit in a circle. One pupil is chosen and, inside or outside the circle, touches every other pupil:

(a) in exactly the same way;
(b) each pupil in a different way;
(c) each pupil in three different ways.

20 This exercise, like the preceding one, can be used with the full class, but is perhaps best introduced in small groups.

One pupil stands at least five yards away from the rest of the group.

Individually (and later in pairs) the pupils walk slowly to the isolated one and touch him in different ways.

(These last two exercises give rise to much spontaneous and charged discussion exposing inter-personal and group relationships. They can easily be progressed into improvised group drama. The journeys and relationships involved are all crucial to the exercises.)

Voice and Speech Exercises

Exercises from the above section can be used for voice and speech. In particular the following exercises respond readily to a substitution of vocal work for movement: Nos. 1, 2, 4, 6, 7, 8, 9, 15 19, 2

Sound-tracks; noises; effects; abstract vocalization; words and sentences can also be used for all the visuals and movement exercises mentioned above.

1 Individually and with a partner pulling funny faces in a mirror.

2 Making "strange" noises: blowing raspberries; squeaking; trilling the tongue; paper and comb music; blowing through split blades of grass; making noises with lips and tongue against the fingers, palm and back of the hand — kissing noises.

3 Making mouth music. Imitate and create "musical" instru-

ments — real and imaginary. (These can be vocal only, or, perhaps later, with the addition of body and instrumental percussion.)

4 Speaking with a fixed expression:
without moving lips;
without moving jaw;
speaking to partner through the side of the mouth (gangster style) so that no one else can see;
speaking with a fixed smile, (*a*) showing the teeth; (*b*) not showing the teeth.

5 The pupils disguise their own voices. They may impersonate or exaggerate other pupils' voices or create new ones. Impersonations may also be taken from radio, television, film, teachers, the headmaster, the prime minister, etc. They may be performed live with everyone else watching; behind screens or blankets; or on tape.

6 The game of Chinese Whispers is played in a circle:
    (*a*) one way only — one sentence from one pupil;
    (*b*) two ways round the circle — still one sentence
          from one pupil;
    (*c*) both ways round the circle — more than one pupil
          sending more than one message.

7 Using the tape-recorder individually, in pairs and in groups to create: sound effects for real and imaginary places; speaking at half and double speed. (The pupils' voices are recorded at normal speed and then played back at double speed. The pupils practise speaking at this double speed. After sufficient practice their voices are recorded while they speak at double speed and then, to check, are played at half the speed at which they were recorded. Alternatively the process is reversed.)

Using one phrase or one sentence the pupils follow one another individually making recordings *imitating and echoing* the voice of the preceding pupil *as accurately as possible.*

A monosyllabic word is recorded a number of times, spoken in exactly the same way, by the teacher or a pupil. The tape is then played backwards. This new (and strange) sound is then practised by the pupils. They record this new "backwards speech" sound. The tape is then reversed to check if the word sounds *in any way like the original.*

8 Making words and phrases work — unearthing maximum variation. The sentence "I like your red gloves" can be spoken in a number of ways:

I	like	your	red	gloves
a	*b*	*c*	*d*	*e*

When individual words are emphasized in this sentence the following meanings are given:

(*a*) speaker does — others may not;
(*b*) affirmation of general meaning;
(*c*) as opposed to the red gloves of other people;
(*d*) as opposed to gloves of other colours;
(*e*) as opposed to other red garments or things.

The following examples should be varied and exaggerated and the pupils encouraged to experiment (to the extreme) in tune; speed; pause; rhythm. By changing rising and falling inflections, statements can be made into questions and questions can be made into statements. The words and phrases that follow can be put to jingle tunes; television advertisement tunes; pop music; Gregorian chants; etc. They can be spoken like machines — with regular beat and monotone. They can be spoken so that the sentence means exactly the opposite of its apparent written meaning.

(*a*) Isolated words:

Yes	No	Go	Come	Stop
Start	Begin	Cease	Please	I
You	We	Us	Sure	Surely
Never	Always	Truth	Truly	Lies
Sincerely	Life	Death	Kill	Murder
Crucify	Peace	War	Super	Heavy
Right	Smashing	Hurray	Hurrah	Hello
Goodbye	Hi	Cheerio		

(*b*) Phrases:

Come in	Go away	I don't know
I do not know	Don't do that	Do not do that
I like you	I don't like you	That's nice
That's nasty	That is nice	That is nasty
There's clever	Well done	I must go
I can't stay	I cannot stay	I wish I could
So nice to have met you		How do you d

(c) The following three sentences from *Macbeth*, Act I, Scene iii:

> "Where hast thou been, sister?"
> "He shall live a man forbid."
> "Look what I have."

(d) Phrases suitable for group work and movement. (The phrases can be used by individuals but in group work the range and contrast of tune, rhythm and echo can be extended.)

Killing swine	Munched and munched and munched
Rump-fed ronyon	In a sieve I'll thither sail
A rat without a tail	I'll give thee a wind
Drain him dry as hay	Dwindle, peak and pine
Tempest-tossed	The weird sisters, hand in hand

4

Playmaking
(Organizing and Manipulating)

HOW PLAYMAKING DIFFERS FROM IMPROVISATION

Improvisation, as outlined in Chapter 2, consists of:
>   journeys of discovery;
>   creative processes which may burn out at any time;
>   self-generating, self-continuing acts which are concerned
>   with personal experience and immediate expression.

The following quotation (my italics) helps illuminate the differences between improvisation and playmaking:

"The *free development* of the powers of imagination must not be restricted. There must be no *canalisation,* no *directives,* no *preconceived* ideas, no *limits.* I believe a genuine work of art is one in which the initial intentions of the artist have been *surpassed:* where the flood of imagination has *swept* through the barriers or out of the narrow channels in which he first tried to confine it: extending beyond *messages,* ideologies and the desire to prove or teach. This *absolute freedom* of the imagination is called escape or evasion by the gloomy critics of our time, whereas it it true creation. To make a new world is to satisfy the insistent demands of a mind that would be stifled if its needs were not fulfilled."[1]

Improvisation is essentially: *free development — surpassing — sweeping — absolute freedom.*

Playmaking is essentially: *canalisation — direction — preconception — limitation — intention — messages* and is made up of:
>   arrivals and destinations;
>   formalized products;
>   disciplines of declared intentions;

[1] *Notes and Counter-notes,* by Eugène Ionesco, 1964. John Calder (Publishers) Ltd., London.

organization and manipulation of language;
communication of intellectual concepts;
surmounting problems;
group expression and the power of recall.

Playmaking is the conscious creation of formalized theatre and as such should not be introduced before the pupils have gained their own necessary understandings of form and discipline in movement, language and theatre.

THE MAIN COMPONENTS

In playmaking the four main components — creating, organizing, doing, observing — can occur in almost any order and also simultaneously. A class may be occupied as a whole unit or in groups; a group within the class may work separately. There is a place for twos and threes as well as for individual work.

Everyone has the opportunity to do something of everything or to specialize, and this choice is an important part of the educative role of playmaking. The contribution each pupil makes and the form in which he makes it are milestones on his journey to maturity.

Some will want to dream; some will want to plan; some will want to organize; some to investigate and some to execute.

Some pupils will choose material that is exciting and some romantic; some will prefer the mundane, some the factual and some the classical. Some will be interested in events and some in people.

These choices reflect the pupils' attitudes and values in life at large. Playmaking — being conscious and formal rather than spontaneous and intuitive — places on the work, and therefore on each individual contribution, the stamp of responsibility.

This confirmation of considered acts and attitudes is another reason why playmaking should not be used until the pupils are at the proper level of personal and group sensitivity and awareness.

Making the play can be compared to the growth of a tree and the text to the seed. The process can use the services of botanists, horticulturists and gardeners. The seed needs a proper proportion of the universal elements to achieve fertile growth. It needs to be nurtured and cared for — protected from over-exposure to the

elements and overgrowth by competing plants. The tree will put
down roots and put out limbs — growing all of a piece — vertically
and horizontally.

Whether head-gardener or not, the teacher will certainly be
something of a director. He represents creator and consumer and
his main task is to draw from the group responses and contribu-
tions relevant to the growth of the play. He is also a teacher of
language — spoken and written, an acting instructor and a drama-
turge. Above all he is a symbolic and constant reminder of focus,
form and purpose.

A BASIC PLAYMAKING PATTERN

There are many possible patterns of playmaking. At one extreme
the play may be written by the group and arranged into a final
script before a word of it has been spoken or any action practised.
At the other, the group may never record a word or note of action
and rely totally on recall from each improvised rehearsal to the
next.

The following pattern outlines a middle-of-the-road method:

First step — decision regarding approach (see below).

Second step— discussion and research with plenty of opportunities to investigate and record (reading and writing are
important at this stage — so is the availability of tape-recorders
and/or cameras, including Polaroid).

Third step — practical experiment in speech and movement
— with tape-recorders and cameras to hand if possible.

Fourth step— further exploration as in (2) according to the
needs exposed in (3). This step will involve selection and
rejection and is a suitable time for early scripting.

Fifth step — further practical realization and experiment.
Previous "casting" will have been voluntary and in self-selective
groups. Changes should now be made so that everyone plays
different roles.

Sixth step — . . . . and so on . . . .

Particular care should be taken when timing the scripting.
Words on paper (especially in print) often achieve a concrete
significance far exceeding any initial intention. They can become
difficult to modify or reject.

STARTING POINTS

No matter which pattern of playmaking is selected (and each group will empirically discover its best *modus operandi*) the decision regarding the first steps is crucial since it inevitably and markedly affects all subsequent stages.

There are many jumping-off points and some important ones are listed below. They can be used individually or in almost any combination or permutation.

1 Character

One or more can be used.

Individuals — fact or fiction; alive or dead; Christ; Gandhi; Luther King; Joan of Arc; Schweitzer; Long John Silver; Malvolio; Fidel Castro; Queen of England; Angela Davis; the Prime Minister; the Headmaster.

Types — divers; astronauts; cowards; enthusiasts; boasters; misers; misogynists; gypsies.

Crowds — a strike meeting; a political rally; train or aircraft passengers; an auction; a crowded employment exchange; spectators at a sports meeting; a television audience.

2 Incident

One or more can be used. In the play itself they can be for:
    Beginning.
    Middle (Climax; Crisis).
    Ending.
An escape; a confrontation; a birth; a death; an embarkation; an arrival; a theft; the discovery of a theft; a loss; the discovery of a loss.

3 Places and Things

Real (from the local environment) — the classroom; the playground; fields and woods. Desks and climbing frames. Rope; stones; tyres; pieces of wood; toys; books; money; matchboxes.

Imaginary and/or Symbolic — a palace; a church; a squalid kitchen; a space station; a desert; a mountain; the bed of the ocean; an island; a planet; a whip; a flag; a cross; a telescope; a bird; an animal; a tree; a gun; a sword; a bus; a boat.

4   Mood and Theme
Hope; Despair; Anxiety; Confidence; Anger; Compassion;
Violence. (Every play is *about* something. The theme is what the
play is about. It is not what happens (narrative) but what it
signifies; not what is said (dialogue) and done but what is *meant.)*

Combinations of these elements can also be used to provide
secondary starters.

(a) Contrast: a (rich/poor) man in a land of (poverty/wealth);
a (machine/man) in a world of (men/machines); a (starving/well-
fed) man in a (well-fed/starving) community; a (peaceful/angry)
man in a (angry/peaceful) crowd.

(b) Story-line: this can vary from an objective, dramatized docu-
mentary to a singular prejudiced position where facts are created
or selected to make a specific point.

The story-line should suggest, implicity or explicitly, the theme
of the play and in the early stages of planning this may mean
events or feelings are injected into or abstracted from the material.

The proposed length is also important in the early stages. Not
as a point of departure so much as a controlling factor.

TWO EXAMPLES
The following gives a breakdown of how points of departure might
be considered for a specific playmaking project. Any one element
is capable of providing the focus for the whole play.

Spain and Peru
(N.B. it is difficult to create a title which is not in itself a starter.)

The main elements of the story are as follows:

In 1525, Huayna Capac, Supreme Inca of the Incas, died and
named as his successor, Huascar. Capac's other son, Atahualpa, was
dissatisfied with this decree. He gathered an army, defeated Huascar and murdered him and all his relatives.

Francisco Pizarro, an uncouth soldier to whom clung the
memory of being a pig-swill boy, got money, soldiers and a fleet
to go to Peru only after much difficulty. He landed in Peru in 1532
and pulled off his coup of kidnapping Atahualpa. A ransom of
Atahualpa's prison cell filled with gold was agreed. When this was
done it was dishonoured by Pizarro.

Although technically released, Atahualpa was never freed. In 1533 he was tried on many charges, found guilty and condemned to be burned alive. He was offered strangulation as an alternative if he would accept Christianity. He was baptized and garrotted on 29 August 1533.

Starting Points stemming from Character

(a) All the supernatural powers involved, be they on the side of the Spaniards or of the Incas, make excellent studies for character. For example, the gods of the Incas — Pachacama; Viracocha; The Sun; The Moon (sister-wife to the Sun); The Stars (called by the Incas the heavenly train of the moon); Venus (known to the Incas as Chasca — page of the Sun); Thunder, Lightning and Rainbows — all of which were of enormous importance to the Incas.

Parallel to this can go a study of the attitudes of the senior and junior members of the Hierarchy of the Roman Catholic Church of the time.

(b) Actual historical characters involved in the incidents are also excellent research starting points for study or character growth. The main characters concerned in the story are: Atahualpa; Huascar (his brother); Huayna Capac (his father). On the side of the Spaniards they were as follows: Francisco Pizarro; Gonzalo, Hernando and Juan (his brothers); Charles V — King of Spain at the time.

(c) A great range of characters involved historically but not known about in detail can also make excellent starters. For example, Spanish and Inca senior courtiers and their families; Spanish and Inca soldiers and sailors and their families; Spanish and Inca lookouts, scouts, messengers, historians and storytellers, etc.

Important Incidents that can be used as Starters

Pizarro raising the needed money, boats and men. This in itself was a challenge and a problem.

Atahualpa at Capac's death-bed, and what was said between them as to how the country should be governed.

The departure of Pizarro from the port as he leaves families behind to go with his soldiers and sailors to Spain.

Atahualpa decides he will take over the country, and in pursuing his aim murders his brother.

Pizarro's first sight of Peru — the Inca's first sight of Pizarro.

Pizarro actually entering the jungle for the first time.

The Incas carefully follow his progress, reporting on his every movement.

They carefully prepare for his arrival.

The first meeting between Pizarro and Atahualpa.

Atahualpa is kidnapped.

The ransom in gold is delivered — but does not save Atahualpa's life.

Atahualpa's death or Pizarro's death.

The return to Spain of any or all of the soldiers/sailors involved in the events could also be the starter for an historical/documentary dramatic survey of the event that lead to their return.

Places and Things to be used as Starters
Many of the places involved in the story have a strong *genius loci* and these can be used to the full in creating atmosphere. The pupils can be involved in actually re-creating with blocks, drapes, painted backcloths, etc., many of the actual places. These can become excellent stimulatory devices. Some important places and things are as follows:

Inca Temples — Spanish Churches.

Inca Palaces/Villages — Spanish Palaces/Villages.

The Incas at sea on the look-out — Pizarro at sea making his journey.

The Incas in the jungle — the Spaniards in the jungle.

Coricancha — the place of gold.

Guns — Swords — Armour — Gold (the making of any or all of these can be an excellent starting point for inexperienced groups who would welcome detailed mimed activity).

Inca clothing and Spanish clothing — their making and wearing.

How the Spaniards wrote about it all — in written language; how the Incas wrote about it all with string, knots and beads.

Moods and Ideas that can be used as Starters
Excitement and sensation.

Fear and anxiety.

Sorrow at death and/or departure.

Health at sea — Health in the jungle.

Discovery; conquest; pride; glory; greed; friendship; intolerance.

Any or all of the above make suitable starting points for explorations that can be focused on to the story of the Incas. The pupils can approach the titles in any way that they wish and the teacher can guide them at an appropriate time into channelling their work to relate to the Inca story.

"The Kraken Wakes" by John Wyndham

Literature already existing in play, poetry or novel form can be amended or adapted to provide a suitable starting stimulus for dramatic work. Scenes from plays can be shortened, expanded, omitted or added to. Events from novels can also be used. In the original text they may be described in detail, mentioned briefly or not touched upon at all. They may be:

    definite;

    probable;

    possible;

    unlikely.

The following suggestions and treatments are taken from *The Kraken Wakes* by John Wyndham.[1] The story tells of strange and powerful beings/things/forces that invade planet Earth and set up a number of headquarters in the deepest parts of the oceans. Almost imperceptibly they put into action plans that defy human understanding and are immune to counteraction or retaliation. Much of the earth is laid waste by flooding as the ice caps melt, and this is only one of the terrifying consequences of the invasion of the planet from outer space. The story is told by a radio-script writer and his wife.

A *Dramatizations from the Text*

    1 The title of the novel itself can be used as a starter. The word "Kraken" may be explained or left as an enigma to stimulate thought amongst pupils. The single word or the full title can be used to promote discussion or immediate practical work. The approach

[1] First published by Michael Joseph in 1953. The page references are taken from the Penguin edition of 1969.

used must depend entirely upon the experience, sensitivity and dramatic intelligence of the class concerned. With some groups, the very title will immediately stimulate them to intensive practical work. With others, much preliminary discussion, writing and/or painting, etc., would be needed before dramatic ideas would begin to emerge.

2   John Wyndham uses a quotation from a poem by Tennyson as an introduction to his novel. This introductory quotation can be used to create a prologue for the play being made by the pupils, or as a basis for a self-contained unit of playmaking taken itself to finished production standard.

The poem is as follows:

> Below the thunders of the upper deep;
> Far, far beneath in the abysmal sea,
> His ancient, dreamless, uninvaded sleep
> The Kraken sleepeth; faintest sunlights flee
> About his shadowy sides: above him swell
> Huge sponges of millennial growth and height
> And far away into the sickly light,
> From many a wondrous grot and secret cell
> Unnumber'd and enormous polypi
> Winnow with giant fins the slumbering green.
> There hath he lain for ages and will lie
> Battening upon huge seaworms in his sleep,
> Until the latter fire shall heat the deep;
> Then once by men and angels to be seen.
> In roaring he shall rise and on the surface die.

3   The opening scene used as a basis for playmaking — self-contained or as an introduction. The author of the novel makes the playmaking task easy — the scene can contain any number of characters from two upwards; the events are intriguing and clearly described; there is basic dialogue for those who may need it (pages 11-13).

4   Dialogue from the opening scene. Pupils are encouraged to change the actual dialogue to suit the group's needs. (It is not *improving* the text but making personal variations to meet individual and group requirements.)

For example: "Mars is looking pretty angry to-night, isn't he? I hope it isn't an omen."

Possible variants:

is looking:	looks, appears, seems, seems to be, has the appearance of, is showing signs of, looms, is apparently, is seemingly, is obviously, is visibly:
pretty:	kind of, sort of, rather, very, quite, fairly, mighty, notably, strikingly, singularly, downright, darned, hell-fired, plaguily.
angry:	foul, wild, furious, mad, troubled, fiery, seeing red, irritable, irate, wrathful, indignant, in a temper, in a huff, taken umbrage, in high dudgeon, hopping mad, hot-blooded.
omen:	sign, portent, augury, token, promise, symbol, emblem, warning, black cat, broken mirror, seven year's bad.

(In each of the examples the variations can be discovered by practical experiment in improvised dialogue or scenes — or as part of "literary research" and written down or tape-recorded) — all exposing subtleties of *meaning and character*.)

5   Radio Commentator's description of disaster at sea (pages 96-98). The scene could be played as a radio or TV broadcast — with or without listeners/viewers. It could be re-enacted with or without the broadcast. It could be played from the homecoming mentioned in the last paragraph, etc.

B   *Dramatizations from events mentioned but not described in the text.*

1   The Destroyed Bathyscope.

At approximately twelve hundred fathoms, in the ocean near the West Indies, the bathyscope is parted from its cable — as a result of intense heat (page 33).

The dramatization can be set on board the ship servicing the bathyscope; in the bathyscope itself; or both, simultaneously. Explaining the fusing of the metal in the circumstances described offers a stimulating challenge.

2   The transatlantic liner Queen Anne is lost at sea (page 89).

The dramatization of the incident can be set on board the

Queen Anne; observed from a helicopter; played exclusively by
the survivors — in their lifeboats, rafts and wreckage — before
and after their rescue. It would make good material for a tape-
recording project — with or without the use of slides.

   3 Parliament is moved from London to Harrogate (pages 217-
      218).

The dramatization can cover the following: the debate on the
proposal to leave London; what to take from Government offices
and files in the emergency; what shall happen to the old Houses of
Parliament; the first assembly in Harrogate; the necessary comman-
deering of property and accommodation in Harrogate.

   4 Navigating flooded London (page 231).

The situation is open to many interpretations.

   5 The laying up of food (pages 233-4).

The building of the arbour and the selection of food to stock
it with are only two items of possible interest.

C *Dramatization from events neither mentioned nor described in*
   the text.

On Mars itself; on the bed of the ocean; in the clouds; on
mountain tops.

   Inside the missiles from Mars.

   Hospitals; the elderly; the blind and infirm; children; dogs.

   The Headquarters of the Armed Forces.

Historical incidents and novels are only two beginning places
for playmaking. Many others are possible:

   News clippings and photographs from the local and national
press.

   General interest articles and photographs (including advertise-
ments) from magazine and colour supplements.

   Music (live and recorded) from a single drum-beat or cymbal-
roll or plucked string to a pop group or symphony orchestra. The
music may or may not be discarded as the playmaking progresses.

   Lighting to create and/or suggest mood and atmosphere.

   Plays, poems, radio, TV and films.

   Improvisations can provide a suitable beginning position for
playmaking. If they are used for this purpose the pupils should
know exactly where and when the pattern changes from creative,

improvised work into channels of organization and manipulation
for specific playmaking, otherwise the improvised work will
appear to have too many restrictions and the playmaking too many
woolly edges.

A Novel Approach

New methods of presenting texts to promote improvisation, playmaking and full-blown productions are gradually appearing on
the educational market. One particular version — "PLAYSCRIPTS"[1]
— should appeal to those teachers who are looking for source
material that specifically sets out to provide a text that can be used
for any or all of the three areas of dramatic activity. They are flexible
texts, with many options for the pupils, that serve as spring-boards
for group and/or classwork, from the simplest exercises to the most
sophisticated productions. They are mentioned at this stage since
they occupy a half-way house between informal exercises and
formal texts.

So far this book has been concerned more with creativity and
expression than with appreciationand interpretation. We now move
on to consider those areas.

[1] For full details contact: Kenyon-Deane Ltd., 129 St John's Hill, London
SW11. Tel: 01—223 3472.

5

Drama from Poetry
(Enriching)

The three areas of reading, writing and talking can, without serious misrepresentation, be equated with the three areas of experience, expression and communication. In English and drama work all three should intermix and intermingle — feeding on and nurturing one another.

Literature, exploring as it does the depth of wealth of the psych has a special role to play. Drama matches that role by furthering th exploration and enabling depth and wealth to be made manifest.

There should be a continuing two-way traffic:
Literature — stimulating and enriching practical drama in all its for
Drama — providing in-depth existential experiences of literature.

Breadth of vocabulary; rhythm and flow; recall and awareness ir the use of language, are all vital to personal development and inter-personal relationships. What is said; where, when and how it is said what is meant and what is remembered all play an important part in everyday life. Literature and drama, working co-operatively, illuminate the use of language and build up the pupils' mastery of it in a unique and powerful manner.

EXERCISES
The following exercises are derived from poems. The approach remains the same for novels (see Chapter 4 "Playmaking") or texts (see Chapter 6 "Using a Text") and the material can be used before, during or after the exercises.

"Boy into Heron," by Celia Randall[1]
High on a stilt-raised bed above the reeds

[1] This poem is reproduced by kind permission of Celia Randall.

He lay and watched the birds, saw the grey heron come,
Perched like himself on long stiff legs,
To search the mud-wet shore for frogs and fish,
Marked his smooth plumage and the deep slate tail,
And the dark coronet of glossy plumes,
And watching so intently, lost himself,
His own identity merged in the bird's.
So when the heron rose above the loch,
His thin legs arrowed in the wind,
His plumes laid flat, the boy took wings,
And rose with him and skimmed across the lake
And knew the majesty and joy of flight.
Not till the heron grew a distant speck
Beyond his sight, did he, reluctant, creep
Into his body's wingless form again.

1 *Movement exercise.* Begin with concentration and absorption on the texture and temperature of mud as a solo exercise in touch. Then progress into pair, group and related work:

Two tribes — one living entirely in cold mud and the other in warm;

Faces covered in mud-packs in beauty-parlours and the strange shapes of all-in wrestlers in mud-baths;

Creatures living in mud or made of mud. (An excellent exercise in control for the inexperienced and in imagination for the more experienced.)

Contrast with people and creatures who have sticks for bones, or stilts for legs or who walk as if their bones were made of glass. Use in conjunction with exercises prompting the feeling of height and tallness, concentrating on a search for elongation through an experience of thinness in the fingers and hands; thinness in the neck and arms and in the toes and feet. Develop the idea of veins and arteries carrying water or nitro-glycerine instead of blood.

2 *Bird-watching and observations through binoculars or telescopes.* This is an activity that can help reinforce the difference between looking and seeing. The visual exercises could be followed by sketching, painting or writing as accurately as possible all the details of what was seen. This could be followed by imaginative

descriptions of what *might* have been seen: in the air; on the soil, in the mud or grass; on or under the water. Consider how and what a heron sees; what it looks for; and how it sets about it. Discuss and create the world under the water that the heron is inspecting — an exploration of being forever cold and/or wet.

3 *One part of the body controlling the rest.* The single part of the body leads the rest of the body until the whole is nothing more than that part — say, the little finger; an ear or a toe. The part leads the rest of the body into strange positions in strange places. Follow-up work might be in dance or in painting: "The person of the — nose, eye, ear" or "In the country of the — finger, thumb, foot."

The pupils will be more prepared to identify with birds after the experience of the single parts of the body above, and will be ready to explore touch and absorption exercises on: sleekness and glossiness in skin texture; the growth of feathers on the hand. The use of plumes for head-dress can be another good way in, and has the additional merit of the fascination of dressing-up. This approach readily leads to a consideration of character as expressed through hair styles and hats.

4 *Dramatic dance on the theme of flight.* Start with a detailed examination of the qualities of a feather or of thistledown (refer to "Prayer Before Birth" by Louis MacNeice). A good growing point for the imagination is the essential difference between the fluffiness of feathers (not mentioned in the poem) and "smooth plumage" and "glossy plumes." This in itself could provide an interesting social-drama theme for improvisation in pairs. One of each pair being the fluffy, feathery type and the other being the smooth, glossy one. (The use of feather-painting could be valuably explored here.)

Musical/percussive accompaniment: the close recording of hands and fingers rubbing on rough cloth give a useful sound — combined with a drum — beaten or stroked. The recordings might be compared with the sounds of butterfly wings and wasp wings being beaten in flight, which are available on Folkways records.

Practical work with hands and fingers to establish the difference between "sleek" and "fluttering." This can progress to movement and dance in pairs using the same parts of the body and then extend to other parts of the body. At almost any time the work can grow from solo to pairs, to small groups to the whole class; always concentrating on contrast.

A possible beginning for dramatic dance on the theme "full-flight" might be in painting and/or sculpture — abstracts which catch the essence of flight. These could be taken into the drama space and used by the class as a basis for improvisation or dance. Other ideas are: flight with or against the wind; Jumbo jets contrasted with gliders — Daedalus and Icarus.

5 *An ability once possessed — now lost.* Begin with personal absorption exercises: sitting, unable to walk, remembering what it was like to be able to walk; eyes closed, being blind, remembering what it was like to be able to see (if this particular exercise is to work well it is important that the children keep their eyes completely closed at the instruction of the teacher, since one flicker of sight can destroy many minutes' preparatory concentration); standing, absolutely still, unable to fly, remembering what it was like to be able to fly (this exercise may be taken in two ways; the situation of an aircraft pilot who no longer is able or permitted to fly; a bird no longer capable of flight). The exercises may be progressed into writing, painting, discussion, dialogue, dramatic dance or improvisation. There is much scope for pair work with emphasis on the contrast between the one who can and the one who cannot.

Another poem that lends itself to practical interpretation is: **"Her Kind" by Anne Sexton**[1]. The poem is read by the pupils in their own time and leads to informal discussion about people who might behave like the woman in the poem: people they know who, although normal, have one or two "odd" habits; people whose relationships with their pets seem intense. This could lead to consideration of relationships between people. "Is anyone entitled to dominate anyone else? — If so, why? . . . .to demand affection? . . . .to own or possess anyone? What gives anyone the right to give orders to people? What is a strong personality? Do any of us treat people as if they were things — or animals as if they were people?" How do we treat other objects of affection — dolls; pets;

[1] Published in *The New Poetry*, edited by Alvarez. (Penguin 1967.) The poem describes the actions of a quite unusual woman.

clothes; money? Improvisation in pairs and groups is a natural development.

1 *Bones; wheels and flames.* Early absorption work on watching the movements of different flames — flickering candles; spurting matches, gas jets. If the class is not experienced it will be best to use fingers and hands only for initial practical work — not overlooking "fingers of flame." ("The Burning of the Leaves" by Laurence Binyon is a useful poem for this stage.) The pupils can express the story of a match — the first burst into flame; the early struggle; the high and fine burning; the final burning-out and dying; the stiff, black stick: — all good material for solo, pair and group work. Recorders and flutes are appropriate instruments for accompanying sound.

More experienced groups can go straight into dramatic dance on the idea of circularity and the continuity of wheels; the brittle fragility of bones and the transience of flames. The ideas could also form a basis for socio-drama in groups of three — each pupil being the kind of person suggested — in thoughts, words, feeling and movement.

2 *"Normal behaviour."* The pupils explore the real meaning of "not a woman, quite." They should be discouraged from dwelling on characters whose behaviour is so bizarre that they might never meet them. They should try to define the almost indefinable in behaviour that makes us feel there is something wrong when meeting this person for the first time. Why is the atmosphere strange and uneasy when all the actions are perfectly normal? (A key phrase might be "It's not what you do, but the way that you do it.") The pupils make detailed examination of any mannerisms that would immediately be noticed and any that might be overlooked. The exercise could be progressed into written work — pinpointing the specific quality and its manifestations in *exact* terms. An exercise of this kind is useful to young people who are trying to work out why some of their most kindly-meant gestures are sometimes apparently misunderstood.

3 *Flames, wheels, rib-cages, nude arms and branches.* The pupils are encouraged to experiment in movement, painting and sculpture, with bits of trees, bark, sticks and old bones of animals and the pure texture of bones (scoured and dried) is compared

with the dried inner wood of a branch. The circularity of wheels and rib-cages compared with waving arms, branches and flames could be a starting point for dramatic dance in a blacked-out space, the only light being the projection of flames, from a slide or moving-effects projector. The pupils can progress from dance straight into painting.

4 *Character work.* Concentration and absorption on the kind of person who can, or thinks she can, feed elves and worms. Pupils may need to decide the size of an elf and what it eats; to consider the physical difficulties of feeding a worm; to work out how to overcome the initial fear of the elves. They might examine the kind of experience in life that would drive anybody in the class to try to feed worms or elves. The idea can also be taken at its symbolic level and the pupils ask themselves what kind of person is suggested by the idea. (It is important to establish that the person concerned is not in any sense insane otherwise there will be no point to the exercise.)

These ideas may be followed by similar thoughts: a person who is obsessively tidy, anxious, accident-prone, etc. The pupils describe and define other things the person might do. After the class has discussed the suggestions, a number of the ideas can be grouped together into an apparently normal person and the pupils work in pairs and small groups on these characters, finding out how they behave together. This could lead to work in speech and be taken to the stage of scripting and recording on tape. For example: "Interviews with eccentrics."

5 *Braver at night when invisible.* Pupils begin with solo concentration exercises on the sensation of weightlessness and transparency; thinness — disappearing into nothingness; a special potion — making all matter transparent. (The pupils might stay absolutely still and imagine that the potion takes effect with every breath.) Concentration, meditation, deep breathing and "potions" should combine to make a strong experience.

A different approach could be through fog: feeling surrounded by and becoming part of black air (heavy air or another type of atmosphere — breathing and moving difficult.) The pupils compare and contrast movement for floating with that for flight. Both are difficult but rewarding and both can be used with beginners to help establish concentration and absorption.

6 *Hands that are unusual.* The pupils concentrate on one
finger-nail and are asked to imagine they can see their nails
actually growing. They progress to a hand with more fingers than
usual; an arm with two hands; a body with three arms; a neck with
two heads. The idea can progress to pairs and small groups creating
strange creatures. These exercises provide excellent stimuli for
improvised music to accompany their movements, especially treated
tape-recordings.

The pupils can also explore the idea in writing: a third hand might
compensate for only one ear or one eye; a third eye for the lack of
the sense of smell. This writing might, in turn, lead to discussion on
what function a brand-new, additional sense might have.

7 *Group improvisation.* The pupils explore situations in caves
— being lost, trapped, hemmed in; caves as places of haven and rest
— protection from marauding animals and the cold of a severe
winter. The idea can be developed into the creation of a society
that decides to retreat from the rest of civilization.

A cave is good for exercises on touch — the special qualities of
darkness and acoustics; wet walls, moss, seaweed, sand, rocks,
stalactites and stalagmites. Reproducing the acoustics of caves is
an interesting exercise for those interested in tape-recorders.

Another approach could stem from people who want to live in
a warm cave and to fill it with special objects. This could lead to
the idea that houses and rooms reflect the personalities of the
people who live in them. It could be continued into writing with
descriptions of people, the rooms they live in and the contents.
The descriptions could be shared among the class and (perhaps
without names being named) brought to life.

A warm cave is also a useful starting idea for relaxation — in
conjunction with soothing water; underground waterfalls; streams
or water gently running down the walls.

A *Solo Improvisation Exercises*
    1 The pupils become characters obsessed with (say) a pet cat.
They sit and watch it over long periods of time until they become:
    (*a*) like it in appearance and behaviour;
    (*b*) possessed by it, and completely under its control.

The pupils try out animal voices and develop them into human voices that can be perfectly understood yet still are, in essence, animal: for example, feline. Tape-recorders are particularly useful for:

(a) creative writing about the character heard on tape;

(b) discussion on how voices had changed, and whether they were recognizable;

(c) solo improvisation: full class creating the movements and gestures as the recorded voice is played back.

(For this last exercise the quality of the recording should be good enough to permit loud playback without hiss or distortion.)

2 *Characters who hoard things.* The pupils decide the kind of things likely to be hoarded. Why it is done; how it is done and where. (Are the objects small and kept in pockets or purses? Are they found — bought — stolen — taken by force — or borrowed? And if so — where? Are they counted and looked at regularly — are they shown off — are they hidden?) The pupils should pay special attention to touching the treasures — feeling and handling.

This can be followed (or introduced) by: movement work on squirrels: sharpness of movements — restricted to short bursts; powers of balance, stillness and control; keenness of features and body shape; the long bushy tail which could be any part of the body — arms, hands or legs growing into feathery bushes; collecting nuts and hoarding them in secret places; becoming accustomed to living inside a tree.

Classroom desks can help the feeling of being cramped become an integral part of the exercise: the use of hands and arms; body shapes that protect things; the use of the desks as "homes for hoarding" (which in fact many desks are).

3 *Being alone: completely cut off.* This can be introduced as a pleasant *or* unpleasant experience. There are a number of possible approaches:

(a) In a hall with blocks or steps, one for each pupil, who is allowed no freedom to leave the block or steps. The exercise must be pursued past the point where it is still "fun" to one where the pupils have a genuine wish and real need to move.

(The square tiles on the floors of many schools provide suitable substitutes.)

(b) In a hall using directional lighting in good blackout. Each pupil has an area of light in which he is confined — small movements only allowed.

(c) In a classroom, varying *(a)* to use chairs and desks instead of blocks. Sitting or standing quite still at desks with hands forming an irremovable anchor or other link with the surface of the desk. (With eyes and ears closed this is also a good exercise in concentration and absorption.)

(d) In a hall or classroom — the whole class moves about the space without touching, speaking to or looking at any one. The exercise then expands "not looking" to cover "not seeing" other pupils. Point out the difference between looking eye to eye and seeing hands or feet as they pass by. Concentrate on looking only at: (i) eyes; (ii) feet; (iii) hands; (iv) backs of necks.

(As introductory improvisations these exercises provide detail for a world of witches and familiars. It should not be necessary to describe any personality traits or peculiarities of behaviour — pupils will draw on these automatically when approaching a related text.)

B *Work in Pairs*

1 The pupils explore the relationship between two people (or one person and an animal, doll, puppet or object). One of the pair possesses, owns or dominates the other. The importance of the work lies not in the commanding itself but in the way command is used. What is the basis of the relationship — is it fear; physical strength; bribery; blackmail?

2 The pupils explore and get lost in caves, pot-holes or cellar-dungeons. They re-create a sense of actuality in the preparation of equipment and in the use of touch and hearing in the dark. They work in pairs as leader and follower, moving about a large space not touching, and keeping in contact by listening only — without touching or speaking and with eyes firmly closed. (Some classes may benefit from having eyes closed but using speech or touch to help.) It is safer at first to have the pupils sitting, squatting or lying on the floor — not standing. In any case the teacher has a busy time ensuring the pupils are in no danger of bumping into one another, the walls or furniture. The pupils must know the teacher will re-

direct them if a collision is likely, otherwise they will open their eyes to make sure. Pairs keep their eyes closed even when changing roles. With experience, pupils are able to find their way about a large hall by concentrating on things like the sound of fluorescent lighting and patches of warmth from sunlight coming through windows.

3 *Contrasting qualities of movement.* One of the pair might take the idea of "crack" and the other "wind." They find suitable sound stimuli and express them in movement. They experiment with the sound qualities of the words themselves — shapes and movements helping to support the variations.

This could lead naturally into character improvisations based on the same contrasting elements and using the movements. The pupils could make masks suggested by the words and later use them to stimulate movement. They could also use mirrors for solo dances to their own masks or hold the masks in the hand or on a stick so that partners could work to them. (With classes of some experience each pupil can dance the mask of partner — while partner is wearing it — and this has obvious attractions for a stage production.)

C *Work in Groups*

1 *Movement* (from B 3 above). The work in pairs can be extended into groups of six or seven and expanded to bring in "waved arm . . . arms," "flames still bite," "ribs crack" and "wheels wind." Introductory work on new images can be done in pairs or in new groups after consolidating group work on "crack" and "wind."

The ideas can be developed and prepared for presentation as a combination of art exhibits, music, choral speech and dramatic dance. The visual side offers challenges for the use of coloured directional lighting to illuminate the exhibition; to heighten the effect of the masks; to provide coloured shadows for the dramatic dance; etc.

Music that contains suitable contrasts:

Goldenburg and Schmuyle	Mussorgsky
The Dance of Job's Comforters	Vaughan Williams
Gesang der Jünglingen	Karlheinz Stockhausen

2 *Creating strange creatures.* The pupils create "group people,"
based on "lonely thing, twelve-fingered, out of mind." Introductory work *within each group* can be solo and then in pairs
with parts of the body taking over from the whole: an eye, an ear,
a finger or a foot. At a later stage the group can grow into one
large hand, head or heart.

D *Classwork*

The class is divided into three groups of ten to twelve; each having
its own working area, rostrum blocks, drapes, lights and music.
Groups work separately at first (solo-pairs-group), then together,
with or without observing one another, and finally in concert. This
should provide a finished product which could be used for performance. A suggested pattern for development is as follows:

Group 1. Take the first verse of the poem and create a picture
in movement and speech of the atmosphere and narrative. Improvisations can be short or long, dependant upon need and suitability
For example, "dreaming evil" could easily be exploded into dramatic dance or speech improvisation lasting ten to fifteen minutes or,
alternatively, started by a still group of three or four figures, lit by
one spot, for no longer than it takes to say the words.

Group 2. Second verse similarly.

Group 3. Third verse similarly.

When the group work is established in basic beginning-middle-
end shape groups come together to share and to run the end of 1.
into the beginning of 2.

The next phase is to bring in fresh stimuli. The aids listed below
may be introduced in any order — but it is inadvisable to introduce
them all at once.

Additional Aids for Group Work
Group 1
Painting by Magritte: "The Red Model."
Music: Recorded: Eastern Sounds, Yusef Lateef. Fontana 688 202
ZL. *Live:* Percussion: Tambor, Tambourine, Side drum, Timpani.
Drapes: Long lengths of coarse black and brown hessian.
Lighting: Directional spots: Open and Canary Yellow filters.
Masks: Full-face masks of one ear, eye or nose, etc.

Group 2
Masks: Life-size dolls of gnomes and elves.
Masks: Half-face masks of near animals.
Lighting: Floods and directional spots: Open and Pale Green.
Drapes: Lengths of blue, green and turquoise silk and satin.
Music: Recorded: Threnody for the Victims of Hiroshima,
Penderecki. VIC 1239. *Live:* Solo and choral vocalization — wail
— plainsong.

Group 3
Lighting: Floods and directional spots: Open and Primary Red.
Ultra-violet flood.
Music: Recorded: The Sound of a Bass, François Rabbath. B 77.973
L. *Live:* Cymbals with wire brushes and sticks.
Drapes: Long lengths of fine white, red and purple cloth
with
Make-up: Arms only — fluorescent white. Body covered in black
drapes.

Related Poems

"Feathers or Lead?"	James Broughton, *The New American Poetry* (Grove Press Inc., New York; Evergreen Books Ltd, London.)
"Prayer to Masks"	Leopold Senghor, *Modern Poetry from Africa* (Penguin)
"Viaticum"	Birago Diop, *Modern Poetry from Africa* (Penguin)
"Adhiambo"	Gabriel Okara, *Poems for Black Africa* (Indiana University Press, Bloomington, London)
"Water Maid"	Christopher Okigbo, *Modern Poetry from Africa* (Penguin)
"Sacrifice"	Christopher Okigbo, *Modern Poetry from Africa* (Penguin)
"The Sorcerer"	A.J.M. Smith, *Penguin Book of Canadian Verse* (Penguin)
"The Great Sea Cucumber"	Gene Baro, *Penguin Book of Animal Verse* (Penguin)

"Pike"	Ted Hughes, *Poets of our Time* (John Murray, London); *The New Poetry* (Penguin)
"Ghosts, Fire, Water"	James Kirkup, *Poets of our Time* (John Murray, London)
"A Mermaiden"	Thomas Hennell, *The Faber Book of Twentieth Century Verse* (Faber)
"The Devil's Waltz"	Sydney Goodsir Smith, *The Faber Book of Twentieth Century Verse* (Faber)

A poem in a different vein but eminently suited to practical interpretation is:

"First Frost" by Andrei Voznesensky[1]

1 *On being cold.* The pupils concentrate first on cold hands and cold feet. It will take time for the *real* sensation to be recalled. It may be best to establish the sensation of cold in one hand only and ensure that this experience is intense. The pupils should feel they are living exclusively through that hand. Once this level has been established it will be easy to move on to the other hand, feet, ankles, wrists, etc.

A likely reaction to having cold hands will be to blow on them: and this will create an opportunity for concentration exercises on feeling one's own breath — warm and cool — on the hands. The exercise demands complete concentration on breath control; distance of hand from mouth; distinction between blowing and breathing — blowing on a burn to soothe it is different from breathing on the hands to warm them. The exercise can be pursued by the pupils working in pairs. The externalization of the blowing/breathing will help create sympathy between pupils — useful in consolidating partner and group sensitivity.

2 *On being exposed to a cold wind.* The exercise may best start with a warm breeze with the temperature gradually dropping. (A strong wind to begin may bring physical expressions which are clichés.) The establishment of the sensation of warm air

[1] Contained in *Anti Worlds* by the author, published by OUP in 1967. The poem describes the first feeling of a cooling friendship.

passing gently over the face first will aid concentration on the fall in temperature which is the main aim. The class is encouraged to explore the room for actual air-currents of differing temperatures — cracks below doors, through window-frames; outlets above radiators.

The exercise can develop into group work, expressing in dance the pupils' feelings about hot air rising and cold air falling. The dance can be varied with the heat source: flickering candle; boiling water; oil-fired furnace; sun-heated tarmac road surfaces; etc. There are opportunities to use different levels; small rostrum blocks; the stage and floor of the hall; steps or other changes of level; personal or group body movement. This difference of level could be accompanied by a rise and fall in music melody or variations in beat and rhythm. The music could be live or recorded and song is equally suitable.

3 *On the idea of loneliness and isolation.* In this exercise, single rostrum blocks, chairs and desks can be used to help the feeling of isolation. The exercise must overcome the natural enjoyment of standing on a superior platform, and the pupils begin to feel the discomfort and anxiety of knowing it is not permitted to come down or to get into touch with anyone else. If lighting is available, pools of cold steel blue light will add to the atmosphere — with or without the rostrum blocks. Circles and squares chalked on the floor can also be used. The essential requirement is that movement away from the prescribed place is not permitted. This directive must be continued until *the discomfort and unease is real — physical and/or mental.* Once this feeling has been established the class might consider what other forces bring feelings of isolation (or claustrophobia); whether people can bring these feelings about in other people without any material or physical aid. What is it about other people or groups that makes us feel "cut-off"?

4 *Making masks*
    her face stained by tears
    and smeared with lipstick.
The masks can be simple or complex. The work can develop on a personal basis with the aid of mirrors; in pairs with one or both wearing masks; in groups with one, a few, or all wearing masks. In

a boys' class or a mixed class the mask can be the mask of a man's
face — this might immediately prompt the questions "What makes
a man cry? And should he? And should he be seen to?" The reference to lipstick can be resolved by thinking of ordinary lips held
in a strange shape or bleeding. Groups might concentrate on eyes
and tears; lips and "lipstick" should free the imagination. The
wearing of the masks could lead to dramatic dance and the masks
themselves could promote discussion on the personae of the masks
of others. Describing the persona of someone's mask in writing
and then discussing it with the maker of the mask is of greatest
value when there has been no previous conversation.

    5 *Speech exercises*
       The first frost of telephone phrases
The phrase can be used to experiment in pairs or small groups with
voices that have the quality of the telephone voice. This may requir
some practical work with portable telephones or small inter-com
units; or the use of the school radio and amplifier. The pupils shoul
listen to radio broadcasters whose photographs are available and try
to determine what makes some of them "look like the voice" and
some not. This could lead to work on "voice-characters" and the
important differences between style and content — especially "Oh,
I didn't mean it like that!" or "What you really mean is. . . ."

    The pupils try to discover what special qualities a "cold" voice
has. This can be followed with situations in pairs or small groups,
working with one character who can say pleasing things in an unpleasant way or with a voice and personality that says nice things
in a nasty way.

    The pupils listen to recorded voices and describe in writing,
painting or sculpture the person who owns the voice. They write
a piece of dialogue for a cold voice and a warm voice; or a piece
which requires a cold voice only. There can be discussion on
whether the written word can ever *require* a special way of speaking.

    6 *On the idea of inner cold.* The pupils pursue the ideas in
(1) to the extreme: in the physical (frost-bite) and the emotional
(blood running cold from fear). They consider people who are
cold inside — cold brain (cool-headed) or cool heart (cold-hearted)
a good or bad thing? Refer to the use of freezing techniques to

preserve living organisms — also corpses, in case remedies are found to bring back life. *The Gift*, by Ronald Duncan, would be a useful text for study; also — "The Snow Queen" by Anderson.

Some Thematic Support Material: "Accident"

The following four examples demonstrate different written approaches to one theme. They can be approached in similar ways to the previous examples. They also offer typical examples of contrasting disciplines which may emerge in creative writing from an improvisation.

ACCIDENT — PERSONAL STYLE

You're driving well. You usually do — take a pride in it. Get a kick from being good. Not fast; not clever; just good. Bloody good, in fact.

Car's going well — engine purring, tyres drumming, 32 miles an hour — 2,000 revs. No need to be in top even. You were more interested in driving well than driving fast.

Like two minutes ago when that fool blew his horn, passed blind, gave you a look and a sign and was gone. You didn't respond. You'd talked yourself out of that — talked yourself into the pride of being good. Any fool could drive fast; but it took real talent to do it well. And that's what you had — real talent.

You checked your safety belt and turned down the music on the radio. You looked at the clock on the dash — you had learned long ago not to use your wrist-watch in the car — not to take chances. That was the trouble with the others — they took chances.

Like the chap in front who hadn't seen the open gate on the off side. Open gates spell trouble. So. . . foot off accelerator — standing by the brake pedal — slow and easy. There it is — the open gate; nothing there; good. Foot back to accelerator — smoothly up to 32. That should have given the other driver time to get away and leave the road clear ahead.

Watch out! There he is again — in the middle of the road, signal flashing, not moving. Right; here we go. Check position. "Exercise proper control over the vehicle and retain a full view of the road and traffic ahead. Change gear in good time — before coming up to the hazard. Avoid hurried or harsh use of the brakes. Look

ahead and brake smoothly." Good. Done all that. "Use the mirror
to check on any traffic behind." All clear there. Right! "Nego-
tiate the hazard." There he goes — turning right. It must have
been the road he wanted. But there's a hell of a fast car coming
— going to pile straight into him. Can't be another car — there
hasn't been time. Unless it's doing ninety. God, it is! It'll hit him
straight on. Head on. No. He's swerving. Going to miss him. No he
isn't. He's caught the back end — a glancing blow — but sufficient.
Sufficient to point him straight at you. Straight at you.

But you were ready — anticipating. You pull on to the verge —
giving him plenty of space. Plenty. But his steering wasn't steering
any more ... bloody fool. . . . . BLOODY FOOL.

"Bloody fool." Funny that — words going round in your mind;
your mind going round in your head; you just sitting there with
everything quiet. No, not quiet; silent. Just you — sitting there
with your mind going round in your head. . . . "Bloody fool". . . .
But where was he? He hit you. Must have. That would account for
the glass and the blood. What blood? Whose? Better get out and
find him. Can't move. You can't move. But it's only the harness
holding you in. You fumble with the catch and try the door. It
won't open. You're trapped. You'll never get out. You'll die in
your car.

The door opens. You feel you are falling. Wobble and float; it's
all wobble and float. Murmurs all round. People all round. Crowds.
Just like an accident — a real accident.

Someone puts a mug of tea in your hands. The mug slips in you
fingers. You look at your fingers and see white stumps. They're no
your fingers. Someone's been messing about with your fingers.
They're white cotton sausages — better get them off. But they
won't come off — won't obey orders.

You sit and think. But you're not sitting. You're flat on your
back with sandpaper in your neck. You try to get your hands to
it, but they're strapped to your sides.

"That's right. Keep your hands down. Don't try to move them.
We shall be there soon. That's right, just you lie still."

Suddenly there's a nurse and an ambulance man. Suddenly
you're on a stretcher in an ambulance. It's not sausages and sandpaper — it's bandages and blankets. You're moving — quite fast

from the sound of the tyres . . . and the engine. . . and the siren.

You hope he's a good driver. Not fast; not clever; just good. Bloody good, in fact.

ACCIDENT — NEWSPAPER STYLE

Two die in A23 crashes

Police are trying to identify two people who died in accidents on the London Road yesterday. First crash was near Rawley, on the northbound carriageway between Southfield Avenue and Orsham Road Roundabout.

The driver of a gold-colour Ford Cortina 1600E died when his car left the road and hit a tree.

Police, appealing for witnesses, are anxious to speak to two men, believed to be doctors, who stopped at the scene.

Second crash was at Laugham six hours later. A car left the road at high speed.

The driver was taken to Laugham Cottage Hospital and was found to have died from an overdose of aspirin. Police believe the man came from London.

ACCIDENT — OBJECTIVE STYLE

DATE: Friday, 29 January, 1974.
TIME: 18.30
WEATHER: Fine and clear. Wind speed 8 - 12 m.p.h.
ROAD CONDITION: 'A' Class Road. Asphalt on concrete. Dry.
NO. OF VEHICLES INVOLVED: Three.

TYPE OF VEHICLES INVOLVED: All saloon cars
TRAFFIC RATE AT TIME: Low and quiet.
SPEED LIMIT: 30 m.p.h.
POSITION OF VEHICLES AT TIME OF ACCIDENT: Two
    travelling north − both stationary − one on nearside verge and
    one on crown of road. One travelling south − estimated speed
    in excess of 30 m.p.h.
NO. OF PERSONS INVOLVED IN ACCIDENT: 6. Two travel-
    ling south, one solo driver travelling north. One party of three
    travelling north.
NO. OF PERSONS INJURED: 6.
NO. OF PERSONS SERIOUSLY INJURED: 3.
NO. OF PERSONS FATALLY INJURED: 2.
POLICE CALLED: Yes.
AMBULANCE CALLED: Yes.
LOCAL FIRST AID CARRIED OUT: Yes.
NAMES AND ADDRESSES OF PARTIES INVOLVED: See con-
    tinuation sheet.
NAMES AND ADDRESSES OF WITNESSES: See continuation
    sheet.
BREATH TEST TAKEN: See hospital report.
ROADWORTHINESS OF VEHICLES INVOLVED: See engineer's
    report.
SUMMARY (noteworthy detail): The vehicles travelling north
    contributed to the accident only by their presence. Theirs was
    an unfortunate and unpredictable involvement. The vehicle
    travelling south was proceeding at an illegal speed and was not
    in the full control of the driver.

ACCIDENT − REQUIEM STYLE

"But that two-handed engine at the door,
Stands ready to smite once, and smite no more."   *(Milton)*

"Speed: 1. − Rapidity of movement
         2. − Success, prosperity
         3. − Hallucinatory drug"   *(Concise Oxford Dictionary)*

   No flowers − by request:
   Donations to Cancer Research.

It was all very civilized and right up-to-date.
The non-denominational humanitarian address
The automated elegance of the process of cremation
The wind-resistant lines of the immaculate white hearse —
All sleekness and skill.

I thought of other sleeknesses and skills
(The car was splendid.
He was young and she was beautiful)
Immaculate automation —
Wind-resistant elegance —
A white, white transport of delight.
Induct; Compress; Ignite; Exhaust;
Burn — but not cremate,
Not quite — and not just yet.

Nor yet the hearse —
Not quite.
(Except and notwithstanding a hearse is a
Vehicle for carrying corpses, a
Car for transporting the dead.)

But in those last lunatic miles
They were in essence —
Dead.
To all intents and purposes
They were already —
Dead.

You cannot contrive a culture wholly devoted to
SPEED
Without
Some chance casualty —
Some operator error.

Instant Society
(chasing the fast buck of immediacy)
Quickly transforms
Johnny Head-in-Air
To

Johnny-on-the-Spot
And the quick so becomes the dead.
In the country of Speed
Acceleration is king.
(The king is dead — long live the betatron!)
And so it was for them
(The car was splendid.
He was young and she was beautiful)

The long low laser of the roads
Came with a built-in starter —
For a speedy getaway;
A swift despatch.
All he had to do was to press the button —
The button marked
Go
Man
Go.
Do your own thing —
Live for each day —
Live for the moment.
Moment of Impact
Moment of Truth
Moment, sure
Momentum, too.
Momentum Mori,
Monument.

This chapter has placed its main emphasis upon the practical
dramatic work that can emerge from literature originally written
in non-dramatic form. It is not suggested that dramatization is the
only way of approaching such literature: that would be unfair
and untrue. It is, however, strongly suggested that dramatization
is one way of exploring more deeply some aspects of that literature — perhaps a short cut, or even the only way for some pupils
at some stages of development. The fact that the dramatizations
stemming from such pieces of literature later come to life in their
own right is nothing but a bonus, and should be treated as such.

6

Using a Text
(Sharing)

Improvisation explores personal experiences and their forms of expression. Playmaking organizes them, gives them definition and stimulates formalized communication. Literature enriches all three areas.

WHAT A TEXT OFFERS
Enrichment from literature through prose and poetry can be experienced and appreciated in isolation and without action but dramatic literature is written for and requires action and practical realization. A dramatic text, therefore, offers *direct stimulus and enrichment through existential experience.*

It works best when the pupils are:
sympathetic and receptive to new experiences
and non-rigid in their responses
because the content of a worthwhile play is:
> original and genuine;
> dense and charged;
> subtle and rational;
> and often:
> novel and challenging.

Its form will appeal:
> initially   — to the intuitive, kinetic and emotional;
> and later   — to the intellectual, aesthetic and rational;

READINESS
Novelty in form and/or content usually shocks — sometimes dramatically (for example the first performances of *Ghosts; Marat/Sade; Hair; Oh Calcutta; Waiting for Godot; The Frogs*). Pupils and

teachers should be able to meet the material in a non-rigid manner and texts should *not be used in depth until all are ready.*

Ready and able to:

> excavate the text — ready in language;
> manipulate the techniques — ready in thought and feeling;
> explore new experiences — ready in responses.

There may be a need for some self-education among teachers. What is shocking to many of them may be commonplace to their pupils. Beauty and obscenity alike (both capable of scratching the human spirit) are in the eye of the beholder.

Action and *Re-action*[1] are two of my plays that have been received with unshocked interest by pupils in and out of schools although many teachers and leaders have been unable to accept them with any calmness of mind. A typical response was that of an incensed youth-leader who walked out of a performance after five minutes complaining the play was inciting the audience to violence. After thirty minutes demonstration that the audience was involved in quiet and thoughtful participation — more attentive than usual in the coffee-bar situation where the performance took place — it was remarked to the youth-leader that the audience was not being violent and appeared not to be provoked. His reply "No — and if they were I'd bloody soon belt 'em" is typical of the rigid responses that can be made before the culture and generation gap can be properly bridged.

The criteria for dramatic literature are not public esteem and commercial success (these can be gained by presentations that are naïve and content that is worthless) but whether it provides:

> delight and wonder

for:

> sophisticate and innocent;
> intellectual and mystic;
> educated and ignorant;
> mature and naïve alike.

APPROACHING A TEXT

Any play script can be tackled in the orthodox manner of rehear-

---

[1] *Re-action* is published in *Second Playbill Two* by Hutchinson's as *Burn-Up.*

sal procedure and, like other forms of literature — poems and novels; can be:

catalyst or trigger;
central companion;
or ultimate goal.

There are three viewpoints from which a text may be tackled.

Reader/Director

The approach is made in private and requires a special insight capable of translating the printed word into a three-dimensional, ritualistic here-and-now realization. (This will most frequently be the role of the teacher. He may also help others undertake the task.)

Actor

This approach is practical and protean — occurring in rehearsal and performance, drawing upon the skills and resources of trained expertise.

Audience

This is essentially a passive though co-operative approach. It can only be appreciated in public performance when its members are prepared for the full impact of a ritual act of theatre. (Like Azdac, in other circumstances, they must be "ready to receive.")

When the pupils are ready, it is important they should have opportunities to experience all three approaches, but it is the last two — doing and sharing — that should be emphasized for optimum educational effect.

(Many theatre companies run programmes for schools. An increasing number of theatres run theatre-in-education services and schemes and there are still the many touring companies — the most known and vested of which is probably Brian Way's Theatre Centre Ltd. Thus sharing the performance of a play from the audience's viewpoint is no longer difficult for any but a few schools.)

Before the text can be performed — the act of theatre created and done — there are lines that must at some time be learned. Pupils may have been prepared for this task through playmaking and this may make the process easier for them. Some pupils may learn best through an improvisatory approach to the lines and others may be happy to commit them to memory by private study at home. There are many views about how, when and where lines should be learned. The final decision must be made by the teacher and the group together. Two factors, however, are important.

1 It is efficient to learn in large, rather than small, measures — pages and paragraphs rather than sentences and phrases. Learning is also best and most efficiently done in a full context. Groups and individuals must, of course, find their own optimum.

2 The writer's words can be used, explored and performed no more and no better than they have been committed to memory.

The major task in excavating a text is to determine from *what the writer says*, and *how he says it*, exactly *what he means*. The same challenge also exists regarding the characters the writer has created.

There is often real conflict between what a stage character says and what he means. This creates much of the meaning and purpose in many good plays. The challenge and conflict can be seen at work in the way we learn about a stage character.

We learn about a character from what he says when he is alone on stage firstly to himself and secondly to the audience. We learn from what he says to other characters individually and in groups — either about themselves or about other characters. We learn from how he responds to other characters individually and in groups and from what he *does* compared with what he says — at the moment or later. We also learn about a character from what other characters say and do to him and about him — in his presence or behind his back.

These conflicts and challenges are well worth pursuing since many life-situations deteriorate because one partner cannot fully grasp what the other means from what is said and what is done. Puncturing the superficial in relationships — on stage or off — is what drama is all about.

One of the most effective ways of doing this and also releasing the latent power of the writer's words is to give those words concrete manifestation in movement, gesture and speech *as soon as possible.* The experiential approach not only saves time but also achieves delights and surprises in the meanings it exposes.

It is an approach particularly suited to dramatic texts because of the final form of their presentation and also because a dramatic text is a combination of:

> Rational ideas expressed through the subtle and precise vehicle of language — appealing to our sophisticated and civilized traits.
>
> Emotional charges expressed through movement, gesture and ritual — appealing to our elemental and primitive traits.

The elements of ritual and sharing are crucial to any act of theatre. The size, shape and constitution of any audience for full class drama should be dictated by the needs of the pupils. Audiences may vary from a few enlightened friends to the class next door or to a large public event. The last, however, is probably best suited to Drama Societies or School Plays and not full class presentations.

The following suggestions all relate to full class involvement and not the smaller, more self-selective groups (drama societies or clubs) embarking on rehearsals for a public production. The main concern of this chapter is with the *process of encountering, engaging and identifying with the text* and not the finished product. A polished production may be a worthwhile spin-off from this process of engagement, but at this stage of full classwork it is incidental.

The approaches outlined in Chapters 3, 4 and 5 are all valid when approaching a play script and may be used without alteration.

With any text, it is useful and interesting to try to communicate the author's original intention through media other than the first form — particularly through the non-verbal in film, photography, painting, music and dance. The attempts to cross forms of communication and aesthetics will illuminate many subtle and exact ideas in the text that may have previously been overlooked or not comprehensively considered. They will also suggest ways and means of dealing with the obvious and basic ideas in the text.

The basic constituents of any scene or play are:

1 character;
2 emotion/mood/atmosphere;
3 incident;

and the three constituents can be abstracted and rearranged to create much exploratory, creative work for full classes.

TREATMENTS

"The Fire-Raisers" by Max Frisch[1]

The following suggestions relate to the closing minutes of Scene Six.

The Biedermanns allow into their house the two strange characters Schmitz and Eisenring. They permit them to stay in their attic although the two are virtually self-confessed fire-raisers, admitting that houses where they have stayed in the past have all gone up in flames. The more extreme they make their statements and intentions, the more does Herr Biedermann try to please them. The extract referred to above comes towards the end of the play, when Biedermann has been entertaining the two fire-raisers to dinner. As the wine flows — the fire grows; in real and symbolic terms.

The scene begins:

"*Schmitz (sings)·* Goosey, Goosey, Gander —"

In the scene the three major constituents are clearly delineated.

1 *The characters are sharp and appear in opposition:*

Gottlieb and Babette Biedermann: they are pretentiously self-righteous compassionate liberals. They self-deceptively rationalize, compromise and temporize their way through life. Their particular brand of liberalism can be easily transmuted into cowardly failure to draw any line of principles.

Schmitz and Eisenring: they are two relaxed and smooth manipulators — easy in their techniques of confidence trickery and sure in their perception and selection of appropriate targets.

2 *Emotion/mood/atmosphere:* a subtle combination of anxiety, bluff and naïvety.

3 *Incident:* the crucial act of handing over the matches is central, simple and symbolic.

The following variations can be used for:

    (*a*) movement and speech exercises;

    (*b*) improvisations;

    (*c*) playmaking;

    (*d*) rehearsal.

(The pupils can be any one of the characters from the scene —

[1] Published in 1962 by Methuen & Co. Ltd, London.

all at the same time — or they can be mixed in any combination.
A full exploration of the personality and traits of one character
by a full class all at the same time can be stimulating, exciting and
enriching. It is a method which gives many opportunities for real
co-operation and sharing at the personal as well as the group level.)

Variation 1. Any or all of the four characters in different situations:

   (a) all four at an auction sale:
     1 bidding together;
     2 bidding against one another.
   (b) all four playing cards:
     1 Gottlieb and Babette *v.* Schmitz and Eisenring;
     2 Gottlieb and Schmitz *v.* Babette and Eisenring.
   (c) at a fair — separately and together;
   (d) in a fire — separately and together;
   (e) in hospital — separately and together.

(First attempts could spring from the exact text and improvisations could promote simple variations on the set scene with
everything constant except some specific details. Later, both mood
and incident can be varied from those in the scene to offer contrasts: for example friendship and trust — an interesting exercise in
conflict.)

Variation 2. Entirely different characters involved in the moods
of the scene — separately or together:
Anxiety; Bluff; Naïvety.

   (a) all the characters different:
     1 parents and children;
     2 police and burglars;
     3 priests and criminals;
     4 teachers and pupils;
     5 members of a secret society;
     6 members of a youth club;
     7 soldiers.
   (b) Gottlieb and Babette with characters not in the play;
   (c) Schmitz and Eisenring with characters not in the play.

The actual incident around which the scene is improvised can
be the same as in the text or can involve money; using the house

telephone; going away; leaving home permanently; meeting someone at a special time or a special place. These, and similar incidents
offer opportunities for bluff and confidence trickery.

Variation 3. Other characters involved in the *incident* of the
matches.
  (a) all the characters different:
      1   all strong characters;
      2   soldiers or coal miners;
      3   convicts or refugees;
      4   revolutionaries or spies.
  (b) Gottlieb and Babette with characters not in the play;
  (c) Schmitz and Eisenring with characters not in the play.
(The mood can be varied for (b) and (c), from the one in the
original scene to a marked contrast: for example joy; co-operation
and/or confidence.)

Variation 4. The scene can be played exactly as written but set
in different environments and conditions. The following are possible variables which can affect the characters and the style of
playing — otherwise the scene stays intact. All the variations would
make a dynamic impact upon the experience and appreciation of
the text.
  (a) *imaginary:*
      1   weather;
      2   temperature;
      3   occupations;
      4   locale;
      5   period;
      6   time of day.
  (b) *real:*
      1   sitting on chairs (or at desks) — not allowed to move;
      2   standing — not allowed to sit;
      3   standing still — not allowed to move;
      4   never being still — always on the move;
      5   standing on desks — or blocks or equivalent — not allowed
           to move from them;
      6   played in coloured directional light;

   7 played against or in projected images;
   8 spoken in whispers only;
   9 spoken in loud voices only;
  10 large gestures only;
  11 small gestures only;
  12 all the characters close to one another;
  13 all the characters far away from one another.

The above mentioned variables can be used:

  (a) for all the characters in the scene;
  (b) for some characters in the scene;
  (c) for only one character in the scene;
  (d) throughout the scene;
  (e) for only part of the scene.

Variation 5. The characters and locale for the scene built up by the following:

    clothes; make-up; masks; properties; furniture.

They can be:

(a) designed and sketched;
(b) discovered through photographs and pictures;
(c) obtained from homes, jumble sales and/or friends;
(d) made.

They can be worn and used:

(a) by the individuals concerned;
(b) shared within a group;
(c) exclusively for the scene of the play;
(d) in exercises; playmaking and improvisations.

The characters themselves can be explored and created by:

(a) collecting and arranging the things:
   1 they own;
   2 they wear;
   3 concerning them (photographs; newspaper reports and magazine articles and features; incidents — all of which the character *would* or *might* have been involved in).
(b) writing about the character and everything in *(a)* above;
(c) painting about the character and everything in *(a)* above;
(d) introducing into exercises; playmaking; improvisations or the text — everything in *(a)* above.

"Macbeth" (the Witches) (Act I, Scene iii)

Thunder. Enter the three Witches

1 Witch.	Where hast thou been, sister?
2 Witch.	Killing swine.
3 Witch.	Sister, where thou?
1 Witch.	A sailor's wife had chestnuts in her lap,
	And munched and munched and munched. "Give me," quoth I.
	"Aroint thee, witch!" the rump-fed ronyon cries.
	Her husband's to Aleppo gone, master o' the *Tiger*
	But in a sieve I'll thither sail,
	And like a rat without a tail
	I'll do, I'll do, and I'll do.
2 Witch.	I'll give thee a wind.
1 Witch.	Th' art kind.
3 Witch.	And I another.
1 Witch.	I myself have all the other.
	And the very ports they blow,
	All the quarters that they know
	I' the shipman's card.
	I'll drain him dry as hay:
	Sleep shall neither night nor day
	Hang upon his penthouse lid;
	He shall live a man forbid;
	Weary sev'n-nights nine times nine
	Shall he dwindle, peak, and pine.
	Though his bark cannot be lost,
	Yet it shall be tempest-tossed.
	Look what I have!
2 Witch.	Show me, show me!
1 Witch.	Here I have a pilot's thumb,
	Wracked as homeward he did come.
	(Drum within.)
3 Witch.	A drum! a drum!
	Macbeth doth come.
All.	The Weird Sisters, hand in hand,
	Posters of the sea and land,

> Thus do go, about, about;
> Thrice to thine, and thrice to mine,
> And thrice again, to make up nine.
> Peace! The charm's wound up.

Although the archetypal nature of the characters offers compelling images, if a performance is to achieve telling validity the essence of contemporary atmosphere and significance must be injected into the scene. The text offers little to bring more than stock responses from any but imaginative and perceptive pupils. Most would fall back upon the clichés of a Welsh Hats and Pimples style.

The pupils need a background of related experience on which to draw before approaching the text — an understanding of those forces in all of us symbolized by the witches.

The following exercises use more than the nominated characters. They may or may not appeal for public presentation, but they provide opportunities for exploring appropriate backgrounds. They can be used as self-contained pieces (growing into finished units without further reference to the play) or as stimuli and signposts *en route* to a full-scale production.

Given below are suggested environments which will help provoke fresh responses and expose challenging incongruities. If the exercises are to work efficiently the pupils must be in complete command of:

(a) their lines;

(b) the environment.

Nothing must stand in the way of the emotional, physical and intellectual stretching that must occur when the exercise bites. Otherwise what was intended to be fresh insight will become unjustified essays in the pretentious and originality and experiment will have degenerated into mere oddness.

(If the setting were a High Court, for example, the rules, roles and rituals sufficient and necessary for the occasion must have been mastered by the pupils or they will stumble over obstacles of procedural techniques.)

Action and text should illuminate one another to provide enriching unity for the cast and enlightenment for the audience.

Some possible environments

1 Coffee Bar.
2 Nurses with Prams in the Park.
3 Whist Drive — Table for Four.
4 Board of Directors — Business Conference.
5 Army Parade or Prison Cell.
6 Bingo Hall — Groups within the Hall.
7 Amusement Arcade with Fruit Machines and Pin-ball Machine
8 Puppet Theatre — dolls and operators.

Variation 1. Groups of six: each witch being taken by two pupils
— one, a puppet and the other a manipulator. The manipulator has
all the initiative, energy and dynamic — does all the thinking,
prompting and arranging — giving instructions to the puppet, who
merely speaks and moves. The control factor can vary: apparent
extra-sensory-perception; the strings of a puppet; eye-to-eye looks
between the two; the puppet on a lead or string. The more subtle
the manipulations the more the pupils will equate them with the
vertical, social relationships they know and understand.

Variation 2. Groups of nine: each witch represented by a group
of three; alternatively, three groups of three, each with three
separate witches. In the first approach, the groups present a com-
posite portrait of each witch. In the second each group contains
within itself three fully developed characters or beings representing
one witch from the text. In both cases words and actions are in unison.

Variation 3. Groups of twelve: three groups of three and a leader
The groups could be arranged as in Variation 2, the leader being an
emissary of the group, presenting its image: a secret society that
will only communicate with the outside world through one remove
for fear of loss of power or "energy." (Attention might be drawn
to the practice in many tribes of refusing to disclose given names
to anyone not in the family or of looking at someone feared or dis-
trusted only by means of a mirror — useful for improvisations
based on eye-to-eye contact and the idea of the "evil eye.")

Variation 4. Any of the above: with the Master of the *Tiger* and
his wife performing the action described in the text. This could be

a visual accompaniment to the action of the witches; or a central action — creatures summoned up by the witches (a similar "calling-up" technique could precede Macbeth, with the lines "A drum, a drum!/Macbeth doth come.")

Variation 5. Any of the above: with rostrum blocks to represent the *Tiger* and lengths of silk or satin to represent the elements that work upon it — the size of cast can very to fit the requirements of the class, from 6 to 36. (With this treatment, as with the others, there are many opportunities for chorus or group dance and vocalization, which could add up to a thirty-minute scene for private viewing or public performance.)

Additionally:

A For classes specially interested in the use of masks and make-up, treatments numbers 1 and 3 above could be adapted as follows:

(a) in pairs: one witch with masks and the other without;

(b) in groups of four: the emissary to be the one with the mask or the only one without.

B For all girl classes the scenes might be: a Beauty Salon; Hair-dressing Salon; Mannequin Parade or Beauty Competition. In each of these there is the opportunity to explore the tension that exists between public image and private self, appearance and reality — there is also merit in examining the forces at work when the stigma of ugliness has been removed from the witches.

C Those classes particularly interested in the visual side might usefully design and create slides, either by painting on to 3 in. square transparencies and projecting them through an optical-effects projector or by painting them in whatever medium, size and shape appeal most and making 35 mm slides for projection through a standard slide projector. The projected images may be used:

(a) as an abstract or natural background for the action;

(b) as supporting material for the action;

(c) an illustrated lecture by one witch, for the education and instruction of the others.

Events: three Miniatures

The following miniatures are typical of material suitable for exercises, improvisations and playmaking. They promote:

(a) exploring relationships;

(b) experimenting with voice and speech techniques to affect the significance of what is said and meant;

(c) experimenting with movement and gesture techniques to affect the significance of what is said and meant;

(d) moving up and down the emotional register;

(e) changing the interior and exterior meanings completely;

(f) varying the emotional overtones relating to the characters and the scene.

Events: Three Miniatures

A.   I've been coming here for years.

B.   So have I.

A.   Years and years.

B.   So have I.

A.   I was happy then.

B.   So was I.

A.   We used to come for picnics. There was a man gave me his apples. Said he couldn't eat them with his teeth. Never knew what he meant. I loved apples. Still do.

B.   So do I.

A.   I never think of this place without thinking of apples. Used to sit and eat them. That's how I think of this place. You know.

B.   I know.

A.   That's why I come here. You know what I mean.

B.   I know what you mean. *(Exit.)*

A.   I knew you would. *(Takes out apple. Sits.)*

"Events" 2

A   enters. Sits.

B   enters. Sits next A.

C   enters. Sits next B.

D   enters. Sits next C. Stands. Moves to A.
     Sits next to him away from B. Whispers to A.

A   whispers to B.

B   whispers to C.

C   stands. Moves to D. Whispers to D. Exit.

They all move up one place.

D stands. Moves next *B* away from *A*. Whispers to *B*.
B whispers to *A*.
A stands. Moves to *D*. Whispers to *D*. Exit.
They move back one place.
D makes a large gesture.
C enters. Sits next *D* away from *B*. Whispers to *D*.
D whispers to *B*.
B stands. Moves next *C* away from *D*. Whispers to *C*.
C & B stand. Whisper together. Exit.
D stands.
D sits.

"Events" 3
A sitting, carving.
B enters, stands watching.
C enters, stands watching.
B (to *C*): He's an archaeologist. I've been watching him for hours.
C. I know. I used to work for him. He's brilliant.
D enters. Stands next *B*.
B (to *D*): He's a brilliant archaeologist. I used to work with him.
C. We both used to work with him.
B. He had to leave his last post. He was too experimental.
C. He made too much progress.
E enters, stands next *D*.
D (to *E*): We've been watching him for hours. He's a brilliant, pro-
       gressive, experimental archaeologist. He used to work for us.
E & A exit together.
B, C & D remain.

"Burn-up" by Derek Bowskill
(An extract from a play written to stimulate a group approach to
presentation.)
All.   Let's get where the fire is.
          Let's go where the fire goes.
   5.   To-day
   6.   I had
   7.   My first. . .
5,6,7 BURN-UP.

All.	BURN-UP!
8.	Bigger than a fiery furnace.
9.	Bigger than a burning witch-hunt.
10.	Better than the KLU-KLUX-KLAN.
11.	And the biggest and best burn-up of all. . .
12.	Fire for sacrifice ——
All.	Sacrifire!
1.	Voodoo — the fire in the blood.
2.	Voodoo — the fire in the soul.
3.	Voodoo — the fire inside.
All.	Voodoo — Voodoo — Voodoo — Voodoo!
4.	*Take a friendship — twist it; break it.*
5.	*Take a kind act — then suspect it.*
All.	*All you need is — malice and envy.*
	All you need is — greed and spite.
6.	*Take an action — turn it, bend it.*
7.	*Take a gesture — then reject it.*
All.	*All you need is — malice and envy.*
	All you need is — greed and spite.
8.	Take a letter — any letter.
9.	Take a letter — letter "A."
10.	A says 'atred;
11.	A says 'ateful;
12.	A says anything you like.
All.	*All you need is — malice and envy.*
	All you need is — greed and spite.
1.	Take a letter — any letter.
2.	Take a letter — letter "B."
3.	Be this;
4.	Be that;
5.	Be off.
6.	B says B-anything you like.
All.	*All you need is — malice and envy.*
	All you need is — greed and spite.
	All you need is — pins and cushions.
	All you need is — candle-light.
6.	Take a cockerel in the left hand,
	Take a sharp knife in the right.

7. Hold the cockerel in the left hand,
   Hold the sharp knife in the right.
8. Strangle cockerel with the left hand,
   Slash the cockerel with the right.
9. It's easy, when you try.

All. *All you need is — malice and envy.*
   All you need is — greed and spite.
   And a little candle-light.

10. There you have it,
    Have Black Magic.
11. Not the chocolates,
    Not the wrappings.
12. Just the dark and gooey centres.
    Soft-centres:

1—3. Dark red jelly — black inside.
4—6. Black inside — dark red jelly.
7—9. Black — magic.
10—

   12. Voo-doo.
       (Then together.)

1—3. Dark red jelly — black inside.
4—6. Black inside — dark red jelly.
7—9. Black — magic.
10—

   12. Voo-doo.
       (The sequence is repeated until a point of dramatic climax is reached and all join in.)

All. Voodoo — Voodoo — Voodoo — Voodoo!

1. I know — it's 19.. *(Insert year.)*
   You're not superstitious.
   Don't believe in witches.
   Don't believe in Voodoo.
   Or Black Magic
2. Well, get this: 19 . . .
   London; England; Sunday; March 29th; 10.30 p.m.
   The initiation of a witch:
   With fire.
   (Here, in low key, are presented some imaginary rites from

*the ceremony of initiating a witch. The ceremony should
contain some of the following: smelling and sniffing, rubbing
oils on the body; touching hands; symbolic eye-to-eye hypno-
sis; back-to-back dancing; erotic dance. The ritual should
gain intensity and pace towards an explosive end. Towards
the end of the ceremony all join in as follows — whispered
at first and gradually gaining in speed and strength.)*

Voices. 1-6: Something's Burning. . .   7-12: I'm on Fire.

1-6: Something's Burning. . .   7-12: I'm on Fire.

1-6: Something's Burning. . .   7-12: I'm on Fire.

1-6: Fire. . .   7-12: Fire.

1-6: Fire. . .   7-12: Fire.

All.   *(double speed):* Fire. Fire. Fire. Fire. FIRE!

(Slow chant): F. I. R. E.

(Drawn-out cheer): FIRE!

3.   O.K. folks, let's try that again — from a Black Mass in London
19.., to a Black Mass in Black Africa. West Africa, 1913. A
young man is going through an initiation ceremony: Taboo.
He will learn the tribe's general taboos and his own private
taboos — above all he will learn that to break a taboo is to die.
TABOO.

*(Drumming begins. VOICE 5 plays the young initiate at
whom all the instructions are aimed. He is powerless and
afraid.)*

4.   Do not eat meat.

All.   You must not eat meat.

4.   Do not touch animals.

All.   You must not touch animals.

4.   Do not fill up a hole in the ground.

All.   You must not fill up a hole in the ground.

4.   Do not watch a death.

All.   You must not watch a death.

4.   Do not touch a corpse.

All.   You must not touch a corpse.

4.   And for you — your own personal, private, special taboo is
never to see your own reflection.

All.   Do not look: You must not look: (Continues.)

(The chanting builds and VOICE 5 joins in. At an appropriate

moment he inserts his new line and everyone is shocked into silence

5.   Do not spit. (*Silence. Pause. The pattern of response is picked up again.*)

5.   Do not spit.

All.   You must not spit.

5.   Do not smoke.

All.   You must not smoke.

5.   Do not shout.

All.   You must not shout. (*Whispered.*)

5.   Do bring enough food.

All.   You must bring enough food.

5.   Do not take bottles or boxes.

All.   You must not take bottles or boxes.

5.   Do not disturb the doctor.

All.   Do not disturb the doctor. (*Continues in quiet rhythmic chant.*)

6.   (*speaking over the chant*): The man who turned the taboos upside-down was one Albert Schweitzer — doctor of Lambarene, West Africa. Self-styled jungle doctor. He did it by white magic — the magic of guts, courage and sheer bloody nerve.

7.   1913.
In the middle of the jungle. . .
The River Ogowe.
750 miles long. . .
Deep, fast and treacherous.
On that river. . .
A canoe,
Paddled by natives.

8.   On that canoe. . .
Dr Albert Schweitzer.
Age: 38.
(*Drumming begins.*)

All.   *Through the jungle; up the river:*
Past the mud huts; past the wood shacks:
Past the palm trees; past the lemon trees:
Past the rotten dying dead trees:

9.   Meeting crocodile and hippopotamus.
       And deadly stinging electric fish —
       Dr Albert Schweitzer.
       Age: 38.
All. Up the river: River Ogowe;
       Through the province: Province of Gabon;
       By the Hill Adolinanango,
       To the town of Lambarene.
       (Drumming begins.)
All. *To the town of Lambarene. To the town of Lambarene.*
       To the town of Lambarene. To the town of Lambarene.
       Lambarene. Lambarene. Lambarene. Lambarene.
       Lambarene. Lambarene. Lambarene. Lambarene.
       (A cymbal crash, or equivalent, to denote the actual jump
       to the river bank.)

There are many ways to approach a text. They differ as one's
position differs, be it reader, actor, teacher, director, designer,
critic. Any approach that is active rather than passive tends to
become complex, since it must draw upon reading, thinking,
feeling and doing all at the same time. This fully-rounded, all-at-
one-blow approach is the one I suggest is the most useful and
appropriate in educational drama/theatre. It aims at assaulting
the pupils by, if not the total experience, something that appro-
ximates closely to it. In these days of psychedelic mass-multi-
media, such an approach is necessary if the properly vital responses are to be triggered in the pupils. I also believe that this
total approach, involving realistic confrontations, frank statements and open counter-statements, is also the key to progress
and growth, not only in the professional theatre, but also in education — in any institution and at any level.

The way in which any teacher brings about the head-on collision between pupils and text is obviously a matter that can only
be solved in the local situation of that teacher and a particular
group of pupils. This chapter has attempted to lay down something of the overall strategy, but really effective tactics can only
and must always be selected, if not indeed created, by the individual teacher.

7

Production
(Performing)

PREPARATIONS

The previous chapters have all dealt with the class situation. We now move on to self-selective groups — the drama club/workshop; the formal dramatic society; those presenting the school play. This chapter deals with possible approaches to public productions and, while there are many permanent clubs and groups that do not perform in public, most of what follows relates specifically to rehearsals and procedures for such events. Groups that do not set out to perform in public may gain something from the methods that follow but their best pattern is to continue along the lines suggested in previous chapters — broadening and deepening as conditions permit.

One of the most important factors in creating the right atmosphere and background for the creative growth of a progressive production is the provision of a permanent home or base for training, rehearsals and performances. It is a problem for many groups to find a permanent suitable place where they can meet regularly and work in reasonable conditions. If the school cannot provide such a facility it is worth while trying to find an old garage or shed — even if it is unheated and draughty. Such a space can offer isolation and room to manoeuvre — two important requirements for drama — very often at little cost. (There is an added advantage if the space needs repair or decoration: the attention needed often helps the development of group identity and sensitivity.)

Reasons for requiring isolation and space are manifold. Here are just a few:

With members who have had no previous experience, a first

step is to gain their trust and confidence. One way to do this is
to use the music they naturally listen to and enjoy. (In any case
song and dance are becoming more and more a feature of contemporary theatre.) The music can range from "greaser beat" to
"progressive" but it is best if close to the current Hit Parade. While
records or tape-recordings are suitable, a live drummer or guitar
player in the group will be an added attraction and amenity. Whatever the style of music, a necessary concomitant will be a high
decibel rating. Hence the first reason for isolation — NOISE.

Noisy music from the charts has additional merits: it provides
an easy transition from their sub-culture to a theatre culture (in
that the two cultures have common ground) and this is encouraging to those who had reservations about "arty-crafty" activities.

Groups like Pink Floyd, Who, Wheels and Wings; interest in
poetry and jazz recitals and the *West Side Story/Hair* idiom make
the use of such music natural and appropriate, and if the group is
to work on improvised movement or dramatic dance, its use is
vital.

The young people likely to attend a drama group or club will
be used to "Sound & Light" discos and stage lighting will speak to
them in their own terms — but terms which also belong to the
theatre. Stage lighting, used imaginatively, can also help relax inhibitions by providing umbrellas of shadow and areas of darkness
or half-light appropriate to the individual's needs.

It is advantageous to leave the lighting in position and a permanent base facilitates this. If the lighting is to be used to full
advantage, there must be adequate blackout. A regular home
makes this an easy proposition.

The use of music, lighting, song and dance are sufficient in
themselves to justify an isolated work-space, but it is also useful
to have rostrum blocks available and to hang on the walls drapes
of contrasting textures and colours. If the group is to use paint;
wood, paper and other materials; chalk, charcoal and polystyrene,
etc., it is important to be able to leave them about without fear
of interference.

Groups are intrigued and stimulated by the presence of mirrors, especially full-length mirrors on the walls. (For many young
people the mirrors are an attraction in themselves and much time

is spent in just looking at reflections. If the initial "peacock" interest is allowed to burn out, the mirrors *help to overcome* inhibitions — not, as is often thought, create them.) Masks; make-up; clothing and acting exercises all benefit from the presence of full-length mirrors. They can be obtained inexpensively from second-hand shops and a permanent home for them is an obvious advantage.

The investment of a lot of money is not needed to create a permanent home for the group, and lavish equipment is not important. What is, is the creation of a *genius loci* so strong that the work place speaks to the group as soon as they enter it. Permanency (home and possession) help create group identity, philosophy and policy — leading towards organization and control by common consent. Since such groups come together because of special and particular aims shared by most members, it seems reasonable to suggest they should be run as co-operatives with every member, at some time during each season, doing something of everything. This not only encourages group unity, identity and sensitivity but also promotes group playing, casting and role exchange — all desirable features of any drama group, no matter what the age range — amateur or professional.

The pursuit of group Identity, Purpose and Style is the best guarantee that the actors' urges will be fulfilled and the audience offered a production to give them delight and wonder. Every stage of preparation and presentation of the play will reflect these aims: choice of play; method of casting; rehearsal procedure; and style of production.

The policy with regard to the audience and place of performance will also be affected.

AUDIENCES

When an audience is invited to share the work prepared and presented by a full class it is right, proper and valid for the audience to be selected for its understanding and sympathy. In a sense the audience is subservient to the cast.

By the time a group or school production (the concern of this chapter) is being considered, the audience should not be selected in such a way. It should be as wide-ranging as possible and should be present for the experience of the play and not because of social, educational or family ties — though there is, of course, nothing wrong with these being capitalized. It is, therefore, most important that groups should not accept into membership *pupils who are not ready for the rigours of production.* Nor should the group itself embark upon a rehearsal schedule until the *group as such is also ready.*

Readiness, at this stage, implies all those qualities mentioned in Chapter 6 and also an expert command of the techniques of flexible, smooth communication — reflecting the needs of the audience the place of performance and the chosen play. It is wisest to move slowly from intimate, semi-private presentations for peers, to large-scale public productions. There is no need to rush. A polished production can be, and often is, a most desirable achievement; but it is no shibboleth or guarantee of significant work within the whole school.

PLACES FOR PERFORMANCE

Plays which tend to appeal to young people tend also to be easily adapted to flexible staging. There is no need to rely on the traditional stage of the traditional school hall. The performances can easily be toured to other schools; youth clubs and centres; old peoples' homes; remand homes; hospitals; community and arts centres; adventure playgrounds (many of them excellent settings for productions); and beaches.

Stage Shapes

The diagrams on pages 125—31 show the range of production shape available.

Shaded areas represent actual acting areas. The arrowed *A*s indicate the audience's seating position and viewing direction.

Page 125 — Sectional views

End Stage — version 1: raised platform for the actors — flat floor for the audience.

End Stage — version 2: floor-level platform for the actors — stepped seating for the audience.

End Stage — version 3: raised platform for the actors — stepped seating for the audience.

In all three diagrams the dotted line indicates the position of a proscenium-type curtain if in use.

Page 126 — Sectional views

Centre Stage — version 1: raised platform for the actors — flat floor for the audience.

Centre Stage — version 2: floor-level platform for the actors — stepped seating for the audience.

Centre Stage — version 3: raised platform for the actors — stepped seating for the audience.

Page 127 — Plans

End Stage — version 1: acting area enclosed by "wing" space and/or changing area — it most typically provides a working area that is hidden from the audience and allows mystery to be created out of their sight.

End Stage — version 2: acting area using the same space as the audience and spanning the full width of the audience area.

End Stage — version 3: acting area using the same space as the audience, but "penned in" to a triangle in one corner. This version is especially suitable to help create "intimacy."

Page 128 — Plans

End Stage — version 4: enclosed acting area with wide, shallow apron in front of proscenium line.

End Stage — version 5: open acting area with protruding apron.

End Stage — version 6: enclosed acting area with deep, narrow apron in front of proscenium line.

Page 129 — Plans

Centre Stages: the essence of all versions is that the audience encloses the actors in the same space as itself by partly (as in 1 and 2) or completely (as in 3) surrounding the acting area. The fully enclosed stage can be a square or a circle (e.g. "theatre-in-the-round").

Page 130 — Plans

These three shapes offer combinations of *Centre to End to Thrust Stages*.

Version 1 allows open and end playing, yet still permits the acting area to be a single entity, provided the distances involved are not too great.

Versions 2 and 3 allow combinations of open and end playing and can, of course, be wider or deeper to choice.

Page 131 — Plans, Space Stages

Some variations for the courageous in which actors and audience share the same space — and perhaps the same furniture, amongst other things. These versions are not recommended for those who do not wish to experiment with direct and intimate audience involvement.

THE ROLE OF THE TEACHER

The teacher/leader's role regarding the production will be that of director and/or production adviser. He may also be a teacher of production techniques.

The essential functions of a director are:

1   To create opportunities for creative growth in the group — individually and collectively.

2   To bring together all the ingredients and methods mentioned in previous chapters.

3   To choose specific stimuli, catalysts and situations to inspire creation, imagination, dedication and execution.

4   To apply that special insight and intelligence mentioned earlier (with regard to reading and/or directing a play) in order to abstract the Theme, Rhythm and Style.

Every play is *about something* — it is that "something" that is the theme. It reflects but transcends the ingredients of time, place, character and narrative.

Rhythm and style are dealt with in detail later in the chapter. At this time it is sufficient to suggest that rhythm is that flow and movement, or the appearance of flow and movement, sufficient and necessary to give a natural impression of life and vitality. The playwright creates this rhythm by his use of dialogue and dramatic action.

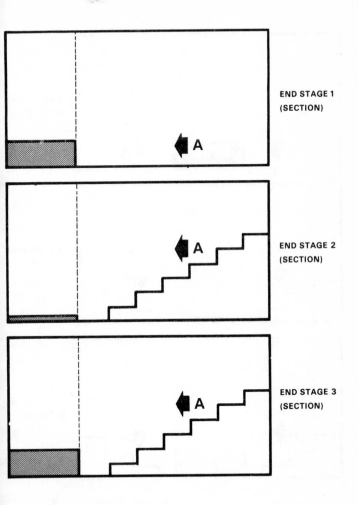

END STAGE 1
(SECTION)

A

END STAGE 2
(SECTION)

A

END STAGE 3
(SECTION)

A

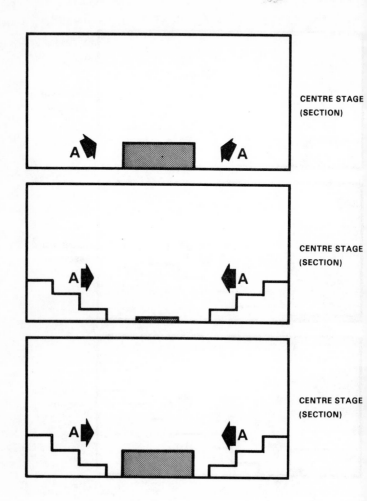

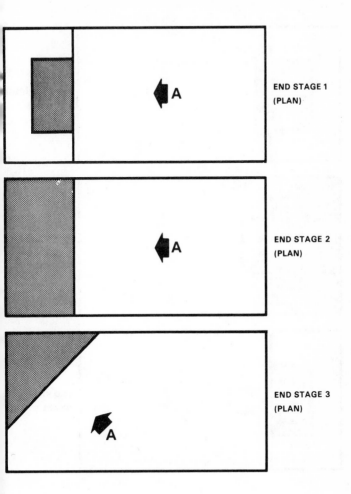

END STAGE 1
(PLAN)

END STAGE 2
(PLAN)

END STAGE 3
(PLAN)

Drama and the Teacher

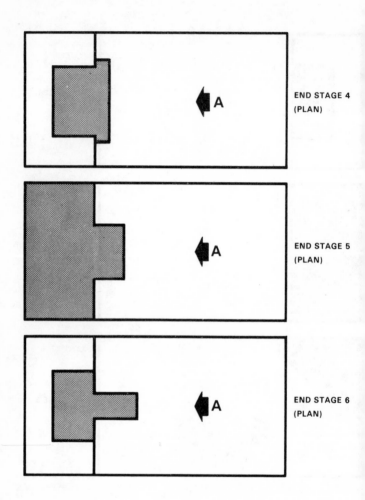

END STAGE 4
(PLAN)

END STAGE 5
(PLAN)

END STAGE 6
(PLAN)

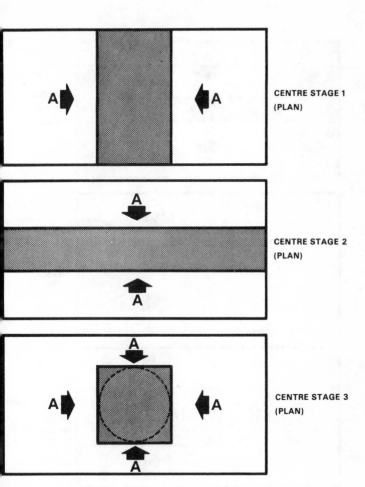

CENTRE STAGE 1
(PLAN)

CENTRE STAGE 2
(PLAN)

CENTRE STAGE 3
(PLAN)

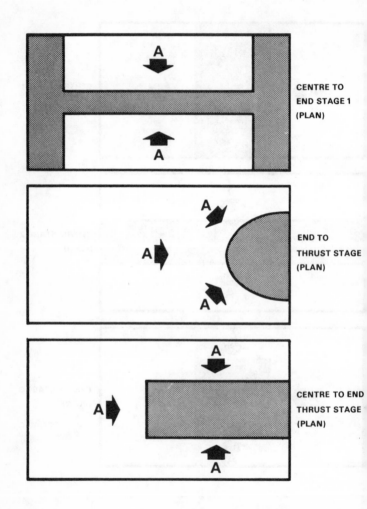

CENTRE TO
END STAGE 1
(PLAN)

END TO
THRUST STAGE
(PLAN)

CENTRE TO END
THRUST STAGE
(PLAN)

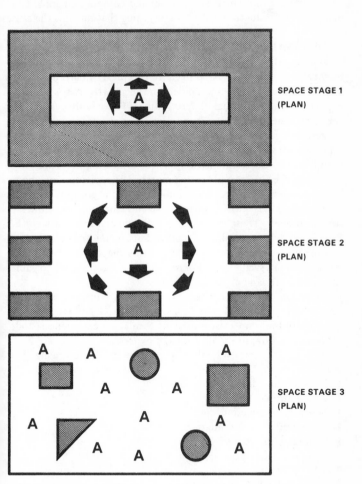

SPACE STAGE 1
(PLAN)

SPACE STAGE 2
(PLAN)

SPACE STAGE 3
(PLAN)

Style also shows itself through dialogue and action and is, basically, the proper marriage of form and content — manner and matter. In a production it covers everything that informs the senses.

REHEARSAL PROCEDURE

Groups and directors must obviously find their own best *modus operandi* but the following procedure is typical of current practice and offers useful guide-lines, based on the growth from kinetic experience to intellectual understanding. (There is always a two-way traffic between gestures and ideas. For example a leader may suggest to a group "wring dry a wet floor-cloth" and expect certain responses within a defined area. The leader may also give the group specific technical instructions about moving the hands, stretching the fingers and tensing muscles. The exercise may be taken at a technical level. Each individual in the group will, however, immediately provide imaginative and emotional overtones for the activity. These may suggest wringing dry a wet dish-cloth. Both approaches are valid in training, but *should not be confused.*) For the pupils who are the concern of this chapter it is best to move from physical expression to intellectual experience to gain the most direct and effective results.

Individual and group pre-rehearsal work will involve reading the play for its overall impact and meaning; research and study; practical work to build up a vocabulary of connected experiences; and the selection of appropriate forms of expression.

Rehearsals themselves will progress through the following stages:
1 Excavation — imagination — creating.
2 Exploration — discovery.
3 Selection — rejection.
4 Acceptance — consolidation — flow.
5 "Running-in" to performance.

A typical rehearsal might run as follows:
Part 1:   Introductory relaxation and physical/vocal limbering.
Part 2:   A short scene (approximately two pages) played, improvised and explored in depth.
Part 3:   Break for relaxation.
Part 4:   The rehearsed scene placed in its context within the play.

The key to the suggested rehearsal procedure is in the "in-depth" rehearsal of short scenes selected for their particular significance:

in the structure of the play;

in the creation of atmosphere;

in the creation of character.

Improvisatory methods should be used at all times throughout the rehearsal to enable the cast to get deeper into the play's theme and machinery. Speech, movement, characters and situations should all be used as a basis for flexible interpretation.

All the elements of design and stage management — music and sound; lighting; properties and costumes; the set — should grow within the production and as part of full group work. They should begin to infiltrate into the group's work from the first rehearsal. This constant introduction of the elements of design and stage management brings continuing feed-back and cross-fertilization between dramatic action and (for example) costume/properties and/or lighting/music.

The design and stage management elements of the production are not to be likened to the final icing on the cake. They are important ingredients for all concerned in the production. Their integration from the first beginnings of the production will not only help create a unified style in production but will also help the growth of group unity and sensitivity.

The essential life of the play however, rests with the playwright's words and the actors who are using them. The technical elements of stage management — desirable to many but necessary to few productions — are mainly support-mechanisms, and the central core of the act of theatre remains in the joining of playwright and actor. This crucial area is examined below through detailed consideration of a play extract from **The Gift, by Ronald Duncan.**[1]

Geraldine. She is right, Daddy. Logically, there is no alternative for you:

If you continue as you are, you will die, as we all die,

With your values tarnished and your hopes dead with you.

[1] Extracts reproduced by kind permission of Ronald Duncan.

You will eventually become as hopeless as we are.
Can't you see we want you to do this, not for your
   good
But for ours?
It's true that today poets and priests look hopeless and
   ridiculous figures
But for all that they are our only points of hope.
We must preserve you somehow.

Percy.   Your logic closes in on me like a prison.

Geraldine. (running to embrace him): Daddy, you know I love
you; you know I shall miss you
And miss the poem you write especially for me
Every Christmas. . . .
I couldn't bear the thought of you dying
And what you stand for dying, too.
That's why I want to preserve you
That's why I want you to step in there.

Madelaine (to Tony).   If anybody can persuade him, she will.
He'll do anything for her.

Tony (bitterly).   I know.

Percy (to Geraldine).   I've already started to write something for
you for next Christmas.
But it's not finished.

Tony.   A poem never is finished
A poem is a point of growth.

Madelaine (aside to Tony).   Clever. *(To Percy)* Well, Percy?
(She gets a pillow.) Shall we make you comfortable?

Percy.   It will be cold in there.

Madelaine (taking his hand).   Colder for us outside when you can
no longer warm us.

Percy (looking at her hand).   That was your best argument.
But I will not get in this thing to preserve myself
Or anything which I stand for:
Either the bad poem I am writing,
Or the good poem I hope one day to write.

Geraldine (petulantly). Oh Daddy. How disappointing!

Madelaine (angrily). What a waste of money!

Percy.   Nor will I get into it to escape from the loneliness

Of growing old, or from the humiliation
Of being old. Or to evade the paralytic stroke,
The fatal motor accident or the cancer we nurture
That takes us unaware: though these fears are real fears.
I will not get into it because I am dying —
Because that it is what we are all doing —
Dying as we wear a new handknitted tie.

Tony. Most disappointing. We shall drop 20 percent on it.

Percy (taking his coat off). But I will get into it because it was
    a gift from your love.

It is that love alone which is worth preserving.
If I stand here, I reject that love
(He steps in.) But in here, I accept it.
It's cold; but not so cold as I feared.
Perhaps it was only my fear that was cold?

Madelaine (handing a scarf to him). Put this on, dear.

Geraldine. Don't be silly, Mother.

Madelaine. And he never had a slice of his cake. *(She goes to cut
    a piece)*

Percy (almost to himself). I can't feel my hands: I cannot feel my
    feet
My closest friends are lost:
It is in our extremities that we are vulnerable;
But what matters, if in our hearts we are secure?
(They gather round.)

Geraldine. Is the thermostat switched on?

Tony. Full.

Tremlett. Not too big, I was wrong there.

Geraldine. Oh Daddy, first recite something to me
Like you used to do when you came to sit on my bed
When I was a girl. Please, Daddy.
Oh, his lips are going blue.

Percy (sitting up). What, darling — one of the odes?
The Ode to a Nightingale?

Geraldine. No. Something of your own —
The poem you were writing for me for Christmas.

Percy. If love is made of words
        Who can love more than I?

If love is all self-love
   Who's more beloved than I?

If love is made of faith
   Who can love less than I?
If love is to submit
   Who's less beloved than I?

If love is made of tears
   Who could love more than she?
If love is to betray
   Who. . . .

(His lips move completing the poem but no sound is emitted.
They lay him down.)

TV set.   Bolton Wanderers   2   Sheffield United   3
         Leeds United   4   Liverpool   3
     . . . . . .*(ad lib. to end)*

(The family now turn to face the audience as though looking
through a window.)

Tony.   Strange: I see they are playing tennis next door
   And sitting out in deck chairs: but I feel cold: very.

Tremlett.   Me too. There the roses lean upon the evening
   But frost feathers my brain, icicles nail my heart
   Now I know what you meant by them mammoths.

Madelaine.   I see my Michaelmas Daisies need tying up
   That proves it is summer still
   Though winter is within us.

Geraldine.   His greenhouse door needs mending.
   (To herself) If love is to betray
   Who was more loved than He?

TV set.   Blackpool   1   Exeter   2
   (etc.)

The Gift of the title is a deep-freeze: a birthday present to
Percy the poet. It is intended to preserve him until "the world is
ready for him." The audience is left to judge whether this
"readiness" would be a state of universal compassion or of in-
sanity. It is also left to decide whether the motives of the characters are what they claim. (Examples of the conflicts between what
is said and what is meant are given later.)

Although the playwright has a built-in justification for his poetic style (by using a poet as central character) the tone and style are set in Madelaine's opening lines:

Madelaine. Doesn't it look pretty?
I think it looks very pretty.
Percy will like this, blue's his favourite colour.
Did you know blue was his favourite colour?
Well, there it is. Doesn't it look magnificent?
Doesn't it?

The use of apparent direct audience address at the end of the play becomes readily acceptable because of the preparation for stylization by the use of formalized language throughout the play. A bridge has been created between naturalism and ritualism.

In *The Cocktail Party* (a verse play) a character says "Do you mind if I quote poetry?". This is an unnecessary and artificial device suggesting the author is not confident of his form.

Poetic drama, properly mastered, needs no self-conscious introduction or facetious mock-apologia. It speaks and works for itself — defining its own terms. Within the well-stated and fully declared form of *The Gift*, even Tremlett's line "Now I know what you meant by them mammoths" is acceptable in form and significant in content — yet still pliable plastic in an actor's mouth.

In the first example given below, the literal meaning contains no element of ambiguity. It is plain and clear. The task of actor and director alike is to explore the possibilities of action and delivery so that the words can be given maximum meaning and the strongest possible charge, while closely approximating to the author's rhythm and style.

The most effective way of achieving these objectives is to experiment with different deliveries of the lines (speed; inflection; accent; pause; etc.) *without undue, conscious thought* about their potential meaning or impact.

Teachers are recommended to try these exercises and examples for themselves, in order to gain a full *body-feel* understanding of the techniques involved. The main principle stems from "Creation by Accident — Art by Design." The feel and sound of the words in the mouth will create meanings (obvious as well as subtle) that

would probably never have emerged from *thinking* about the lines
as they appear on the printed page. The examples that follow will
be of greatest benefit if they are tackled *straight away* and *out
loud.* — by teachers and pupils.

A

Geraldine. If you continue as you are, you will die, as we all die,
     With your values *tarnished* and *your hopes dead* with you.

Speed: (a) Speak the lines as fast as possible up to the following
words — then speak them as slowly as possible to the end. (Take
care not to alter the pitch or volume of the speed changes.)

> 1 tarnished;
> 2 your;
> 3 hopes;
> 4 dead.

>> *(b)* 1 Accelerate noticeably from the beginning to the end.
>>   2 Decelerate noticeably from the beginning to the end.
>>   3 Accelerate noticeably to "as we all die," then decele-
>>   rate to the end.
>>   4 Decelerate noticeably to "as we all die," then accele-
>>   rate to the end.

Pitch: Repeat the exercises above, varying the *pitch* instead of the
speed. (Take care not to alter the speed or volume as the pitch
changes.) —

Volume: Repeat the exercises varying the *volume* instead of the
pitch. (Take care not to alter the pitch or speed as the volume
changes.)

Then:

Repeat the exercises combining variations in:

> *(a)* Speed and volume:
>   1 both increasing and/or decreasing together;
>   2 in opposition.
> *(b)* Speed and pitch:
>   as in 1 and 2 in *(a)* above.
> *(c)* Pitch and volume:
>   as in 1 and 2 in *(a)* above.
> *(d)* Speed, pitch and volume:
>   as in 1 and 2 in *(a)* above.

Pause: Speak the lines, taking the longest possible pauses at the places marked. (Take care not to let the use of pause affect the emphasis on words or vowels.)

"If . . . you continue as you are . . . you will die . . . as we all die . . . with your values tarnished . . . and your hopes dead with you."

"If you . . . continue as you are you will . . . die as we all die with your values tarnished and your hopes . . . dead with you."

"If you continue as you are you will . . . die as we all . . . die . . . with your values tarnished and your hopes dead with you."

"If you continue as you are you will die as we all die with your . . . values tarnished and your . . . hopes dead . . . with you."

Emphasis: Speak the lines emphasizing the words as marked (take care not to let the use of emphasis affect pause):

"*You* will die, as *we* all die."

"You *will* die, as we *all* die."

"You will *die,* as we all *die.*"

"You will die, *as we all* die."

"*You* will die, as we *all* die."

Then: combine the variations of Pause and Emphasis.

B

Geraldine:

"I couldn't bear the thought of you dying
And what you stand for dying, too.
That's why I want to preserve you
That's why I want you to step in there."

Repeat the exercises as in *A,* above. Use the following specifics:

Speed:

(a) 1 I want to
2 preserve you
3 that's why I
4 want you to
5 step in

(b) 3 (i) dying to
(ii) preserve you
4 (i) dying to
(ii) preserve you

Pause:

"I couldn't . . . bear the thought . . . of you dying . . . and what

you stand for . . . dying, too."
    "I couldn't bear the thought of . . . you . . . dying . . . and what
you stand for . . . dying, too."
    "I couldn't bear the . . . thought of you dying and what you stand
for . . . dying, too."
    "I couldn't bear the thought of you dying and what you . . . stand
for . . . dying, too."

Emphasis:
    "*That's* why I want you to step in there."
    "That's why *I* want you to *step* in there."
    "That's *why* I want *you* to step in there."
    "That's why I *want* you to step in *there.*"
    "That's *why I want you* to *step in there.*"

C
    Repeat some of the exercises with the following lines, noting
carefully the build up of character and interrelationships caused
by the differences in rhythm, form and content, exposing contrasts
between what is said and meant dependent upon the character
spoken to.

Madelaine (to Tony). If anybody can persuade him, she will.
    He'll do anything for her.

Madelaine (taking his hand). Colder for us outside when you can
    no longer warm us.

Tony.   Most disappointing. We shall drop 20 percent on it.

Tony.   A poem never is finished
    A poem is a point of growth.

D
    Repeat some of the exercises with the two lines of Tremlett's —
noting in particular the opportunities for comedy or compassion.
    "Not too big, I was wrong there."

    "Now I know what you meant by them mammoths."

E

Percy. If I stand here, I reject that love
    (He steps in.) But in here, I accept it.
    The above is an example of *dramatic action* — movement, suffi-

cient and necessary to the text: often isolated; highlighted and symbolic.

Practise the following variations in the timing of the actual *step* together with some of the preceding text exercises:

1   Step into the deep-freeze and become still before the word "But."

2   Step into the deep-freeze and become still after "But" and before "in here."

3   Step into the deep-freeze and become still after "here."

4   Step into the deep-freeze and become still after "I."

5   Step into the deep-freeze and become still after "accept it."

F

Madelaine (aside to Tony). Clever. *(To Percy.)* Well, Percy?
     (She gets a pillow.)   Shall we make you comfortable?

Madelaine (handing a scarf to him). Put this on, dear.

These are two examples of *stage business*, that is, movement supportive to the text. It usually accompanies the text and although often expanded and highlighted, it is not *necessary*, as is dramatic action. Stage business is usually behaviouristic or naturalistic rather than symbolic.

Practise the following variations together with some of the preceding text exercises:

1   *Madelaine (to Percy).* Well, Percy? *(She gets a pillow.)* Shall we
     make you comfortable?

(a) A long journey for the pillow — speak the lines when at the pillow and distant from the deep-freeze.

(b) A long journey for the pillow — returning with it and speaking close to the deep-freeze.

(c) Gathering up the pillow from nearby before speaking.

(d) Gathering up the pillow from nearby while speaking.

(e) Gathering up the pillow from nearby after speaking.

(f) Gathering up the pillow after "Well Percy?"

(g) Gathering up the pillow after "shall we."

(h) Gathering up the pillow after "make you."

(j) Vary the accent on the word "comfortable":

   (i)   *Com*fortable — along a drawn-out dwelling on the
          first vowel sound.

   (ii) Cumftbl (or even maykiacumftbl).

     (*iii*)   Com-for-ta-ble (pseudo-French accent).
     (*iv*)   Com-for-ta-ble (each syllable short, sharp and equal).
     (*v*)   Comforta*ble* (elongated, final syllable).

2 *Madelaine (handing a scarf to him)*. Put this on, dear.

(*a*) Practise with a miniature scarf.

(*b*) Practise with a huge scarf.

(*c*) Holding it out in front — but away from the deep-freeze.

(*d*) Handing it across the threshold of the deep-freeze.

(*e*) Stepping across the threshold of the deep-freeze holding the scarf.

(*f*) Going into the deep-freeze with the scarf.

(*g*) Wrap the scarf round Percy — one wrap for each of the four words.

G

1 Experiment with improvisatory scenes involving a marked contrast of speech styles as in (*C*) above — in form and content.

2 Use stick-masks to assist. For example: up for poetry — down for prose; up for lies — down for truth; or vice versa.

H

    Place the characters in different situations from those in the play — separately and together as a family:

1 Breakfast on the day of the play.

2 Supper the night before.

3 Supper after one of Percy's days at the bank.

4 Supper after one of Percy's days out after he has left the bank.

5 Meals in the house as the days, weeks and years go by.

    (Does Percy stay there? Does he become like an icon to the family?)

6 Create some of the scenes that are described or mentioned in the text:

(*a*) "He resigned from his job at the bank."

(*b*) "Ever since that day, when he marched in here one afternoon,
     With his valise full of poems which he blandly admitted
     That he had written in the bank's time and on the tills
     And announced that he had resigned his job
     Because he had suddenly realised that he'd misspent his life
     Counting bits of paper there,

And that he was now going to devote the rest of his days
To important things . . . "
(c) "His manic depressive-moods fluctuated between such
Irrational irreconcilable extremities. . . .
His moments of despair were reasonable enough;
Few of us can see any hope.
To me it's his moods of joyful optimism
Which prove he's now completely ga-ga."
(d) Percy. I have stood all the afternoon in the High Street
Outside the bank, my bank.
And I sang (Schubert of course)
And I gave a five pound note to everybody who stopped to
give me a penny.
It was a wonderful business. You should have seen their faces.
Two women kissed me from gratitude.

Percy. Not quite. I've enough for tomorrow too. People seemed
most grateful. I daresay they'd overspent
On their summer holidays. Of course some thought my
notes were counterfeit
They took them into the bank and were soon disabused
Because I'd drawn them out from there this morning.
And there were one or two who paused before they folded
the note into their wallet.
These may in time realise that I was not merely giving
away fivers
But values.
(e) With this last exercise, for added interest use extracts to
create locale and character from writers such as Raymond Chandler,
Ed McBain and Dashiell Hammett.

I

Experiment with the creation and integration (counterpoint) of
sound accompaniments from the radio and TV mentioned in the
script, on tape-recorders. For example: news bulletins; weather
news; commercials; jingles. (Create a special commercial for a deep-
freeze.)
(a) Use them throughout the scene at varying volumes.

(*b*) Use them occasionally during the scene to make specific dramatic points.

J

Experiment with the design of the deep-freeze using:

1   a pool of light;
2   a rostrum block (with or without a pool of light);
3   scaffolding or a cage made of similar materials;
4   naturalistic representation (emphasis on neon-type interior lighting);
5   a projected image on screen. As Percy walks into the picture, it is printed on him.

Appendix I
Checklist: Performing a Play

Copyright. All plays are protected by copyright and no change may be made in the text without permission from the author or his agent.

Licences. No performance may be given without the necessary licence. These are generally obtained from the author's agent, whose name and address will figure in the first few pages of the published text. The licence to perform should be obtained well in advance of the planned production date, since some agents will not issue one if it was not applied for prior to rehearsal.

Royalties. Royalties must be paid for all public performances and when requesting a licence it is important to specify the conditions under which the play will be given (reading; rehearsed reading; small invited audience; school hall; public hall; etc.) since a reduction in the usual fee may be granted.

Safety. Whatever form of staging is adopted there are certain regulations to be met. Local requirements vary considerably and groups should take advice from their Fire Officer. Many of the statutory regulations are out of date and bear little relevance to theatre arts, but they carry the backing of the law and must be respected. Groups should do everything in their power to ensure that outdated requirements are changed, although Local Authorities are slow to understand and slower to change.

Important matters for any group are:

1 Easy entrance and exit to and from all parts of the stage and auditorium — including the case of fire or other emergency.

2 Maximum precautions against accidental fire and in the use of inflammable materials.

3 Areas of special fire risk made separate.
4 Provision of emergency lighting.
5 Provision of ample means of fire extinction.
6 Provision of proper first-aid facilities.

These precautions are all necessary and no group would object to them. Local requirements may be well in excess of any or all of them and the Local Authority should be contacted well in time. It is unfortunate if a Fire Officer feels it necessary to intervene on the first night and forbid the production to continue.

Dress Rehearsals. At dress rehearsal stage the director should leave the production in the hands of the Stage Manager, the back-stage crew and the cast. He should also leave all audience matters in the hands of the Front of House Staff.

The Stage Manager should be in complete charge. His responsibility covers full liaison with all dressing rooms, front-of-house staff, lighting — including house lights — staff, stage crew and cast. He should:

1 Treat all dress rehearsals as performances.
2 Check and recheck with everyone responsible for a section of the production.
3 Have everything ready well in advance. The stage should be ready at least 30 minutes before the performance begins.
4 Never fuss.
5 Be aware of the need for safety at all times.

Hall. Check on your Local Authority licensing regulations and requirements for public performances in the hall you are to use for production.

Last word. Don't worry! Anxiety breeds anxiety and the director should appear to be sympathetic, calm and confident.

Appendix II
Useful Books

General

Angeloglou, Maggie. *A History of Make-up.* (1970)

Aspden, George. *Model Making in Paper, Board and Metal.* (1964)

Bentham, Frederic. *The Art of Stage Lighting.* Pitman, London, 1968.

Bowskill, Derek. *Acting and Stagecraft Made Simple.* W.H. Allen, London, 1973.

Bullard, Audrey. *Improve your Speech.* Blond, London, 1967.

Burton, Peter, and Lane, John. *New Directions.* Methuen, London. 1970.

Clark, Brian. *Group Theatre.* Pitman, London, 1972.

d'Arbeloff, Natalie. *An Artist's Workbook: line, shape, volume, light.* Studio Vista, 1969.

d'Arbeloff, Natalie and Yates, Jack. *Creating in Collage.* Studio Vista, 1967.

Ellis-Fermor, Una. *The Frontiers of Drama.* Methuen, London, 1964.

Esslin, Martin. *The Theatre of the Absurb.* Penguin, London, 1970.

Evans, James Roose. *Experimental Theatre.* Studio Vista, 1970.

Grotowski, Jerzy. *Towards a Poor Theatre.* Methuen, London, 1969.

Hodgson, John, and Richards, Ernest. *Improvisation.* Methuen, London, 1966.

Jackson, Sheila. *Simple Stage Costumes.* Studio Vista, 1968.

Joseph, Stephen. *New Theatre Forms.* Pitman, London, 1968.

Kenton, Warren. *Stage Properties and How to Make Them.* Pitman, London, 1967.

Kostelanetz, Richard. *The Theatre of Mixed Means.* Pitman, London, 1970.

Marowitz, Charles, and Trussler, Simon (Eds.). *Theatre at Work.* Methuen, London, 1967.

Motley. *Designing and Making Stage Costumes.* Studio Vista, 19

Newton, Robert. *Exercise Improvisation.* J.G. Miller, London, 1960.

Oliver, Charles. *Anatomy and Perspective: the fundamentals of figure drawing.* (1971)

Percival, John. *Modern Ballet.* (1970)

Pilbrow, Richard. *Stage Lighting.* (1971)

Portchmouth, John. *Creative Crafts for Today.* (1969)

Pronko, Leonard. *Avant-Garde: The Experimental Theatre in France.* Cambridge University Press, London, 1962.

Rendle, Adrian. *Everyman and his Theatre.* Pitman, London, 1968.

Roberts, Peter. *Theatre in Britain.* Pitman, 1973.

Taylor, John Russell. *Anger and After.* Methuen, London, 1969.

Tomkins, Julia. *Stage Costumes and How to Make them.* Pitman London, 1969.

Warre, Michael. *Designing and Making Stage Scenery.* (1966)

White, Edwin. *Problems of Acting and Production.* Pitman, London, 1966.

Williams, Raymond. *Drama in Performance.* Watts, London, 1968.

Drama in Education

Adland, David. *Group Approach to Drama.* Longmans, 1964.

Alington, A.F. *Drama and Education.* Blackwell, 1961.

Hodgson, John, and Banham, Martin. *Drama in Education.* Pitman. (Annually)

Pemberton-Billing, R.D. and Clegg, J.D. *Teaching Drama.* University of London Press, 1965.

Slade, Peter. *Child Drama.* University of London Press, 1954.

Way, Brian. *Three Plays for the Open Stage.* Pitman, 1958.

Way, Brian. *Development through Drama.* Longmans, London, 1967.

Wiles, John, and Garrard, Alan. *Leap to Life.* Chatto and Windus, 1965.

Myths and Legends.
General.
Everyman Dictionary of Non-Classical Mythology. J.M. Dent, London, and E.P. Dutton, New York, 1952.
Egyptian
Ions, Veronica. *Egyptian Mythology.* Paul Hamlyn, Feltham, 1968.
Assyro-Babylonian
Sanders, N.K. (trans.) *The Epic of Gilgamesh.* Penguin Classics, Harmondsworth, 1960.
Greek
Graves, Robert. *The Greek Myths.* 2 Vols. Penguin Books, Harmondsworth, 1948.
Roman
Grant, Michael. *Myths of the Greeks and Romans.* Weidenfeld & Nicholson, London, 1962.
Warner, Rex. *Men and Gods.* Penguin Books, Harmondsworth, 1952.
Celtic
Jones, T. & G. (trans.) *The Mabinogion.* J.M. Dent, London, and E.P. Dutton, New York, 1963.
Ross, Anne. *Pagan Celtic Britain.* Routledge & Kegan Paul, London, and Columbia Univ. Press, New York, 1967.
Teutonic
Ellis, Davidson, H.R. *Gods and Myths of Northern Europe.* Penguin Books, Harmondsworth, 1964.
Slavonic
Downing, C. *Russian Tales and Legends.* Oxford Univ. Press, 1956.
Ancient Persian
Vermaseren, M.J. *Mithras, the secret god.* Methuen, London, 1963.
Indian
Ions, Veronica, *Indian Mythology.* Paul Hamlyn, Feltham, 1967.
Chinese
Watson, W. *China.* Thames & Hudson, London, 1961.
Japanese
Kidder, J.E. *Japan.* Thames and Hudson, London, 1959.

The Two Americas
> Mason, J.A. *The Ancient Civilisations of Peru.* Penguin Books,
> Harmondsworth, 1957.
> Vaillant, G.C. *The Aztecs of Mexico.* Penguin Books, Harmonds
> worth, 1952.

Oceanic
> Poignant, Roslyn. *Oceanic Mythology.* Paul Hamlyn, Feltham,
> 1968.

African
> Itayemi, P. and Gurrey, P. *Folk Tales and Fables.* Penguin
> Africa Series, Harmondsworth, 1953.

Appendix III
Useful Names and Addresses

Suppliers
SAMUEL FRENCH LTD: 26 Southampton St, Strand, London
WC2.
Tel. 01-836 7513.
Books and plays — acting editions.
Sound effects — disc and tape.
Guides to play selection — free on request.

W.J. FURSE & CO. LTD: Theatre Division, Traffic St, Nottingham,
NG2 1NF. Tel. 0602-88213.
Stage lighting and other equipment — for sale or hire. Not only
will they create, supply and service equipment but they also offer
a first-class advisory service and will prepare notes, schemes, technical drawings and specifications for clients. No inquiry is too
small.

They have branches at:
National House, 131 King St, London W6.
Bramcote, Brent Knoll, Highbridge, Somerset.
8 Hertford Drive, Tyldesley, Nr. Manchester.
5 Hertford Place, Peterlee, County Durham.
205 Bath St., Glasgow, C2. Scotland.

CHARLES H. FOX LTD: 25 Shelton St, London WC2H 9HX.
Tel. 01-240 3111.
A headquarters for make-up, costumes, wigs, armour and
jewellery (sale and hire) with an excellent advisory support service. The full range of Leichner make-up is always in stock.

Publications
Amateur Stage: available from 1 Hawthornedene Rd, Hayes,
Bromley, Kent.
    Tel. 01-462 6461. 15p monthly; £2 annual subscription.

Brochures
The following contain much useful introductory reading. They
are currently available from Stacey Publications, who also carry
many titles on Drama and Theatre in Education.

    Stage Make-up.
    Your Problems Solved.
    The Play Produced.
    Stage Lighting for Clubs and Schools.
    Plays of 1966–1971. (Six separate brochures.)
    Broadsheet: available from London School's Drama Associa-
        tion, 31 Wyatt Rd, London E7 9ND. Price 20p.
    Creative Drama: available from Educational Drama Associa-
        tion, Drama Centre, Rea St, Birmingham 5. Twice yearly.
        40p annual subscription.
    Drama: Published by the British Drama League, 8 Fitzroy
        Square, London W1. Quarterly, 25p. (free to members).
    Plays and Players: available from 75 Victoria St, London
        SW1. Monthly. For the general playgoer, 35p.
    Theatre Directory: An Amateur Stage Handbook, listing ser-
        vices, suppliers and organizations: available at 20p from
        Stacey Publications, 1 Hawthorndene Road, Hayes, Brom-
        ley, Kent. Tel. 01-462 6461.
        Roy Stacey is also the publisher of *Amateur Stage* and of
        Amateur Stage Handbooks covering all aspects of amateur
        theatre – adult, youth and educational.
    British Theatre Directory (annual): A guide to theatres in Lon-
        don and the Provinces also listing services, suppliers and
        organizations. Future editions will include greater cover of
        material of interest to amateurs and educationalists. £1.00
        from Vance-Offord (Publications) Ltd, 1 Susans Road,
        Eastbourne. Tel. 0323-24334.

Organizations
British Amateur Drama Association, Orbis, Youlgrave, Nr. Bake-
    well, Derby.

British Children's Theatre Association, B.R. Whiteley, 41 Church Lane, Normanton, Yorks., WF6 1EZ.

Drama Association of Wales, Mrs E.V. Williams, 2 Cathedral Road, Cardiff.

Drama Board, 20 Beaumont St, Oxford.

Educational Drama Association, Drama Centre, Rea St., South, Birmingham 5.

Guild of Drama Adjudicators, 26 Bedford Square, London, WC1.

Radius: Religious Drama Society of Great Britain, George Bell House, Bishop's Hall, Ayres St, London S.E.1.

Society of Teachers of Speech & Drama, 82 St John's Rd, Sevenoaks, Kent.

The British Theatre Association.

Director: Walter Lucas, 9/10 Fitzroy Square, London WIP 6AE. Tel. 01-387 2666.

"To assist the Development of the art of the Theatre and to promote a right relation between Drama and the life of the community."

The British Theatre Association is, essentially, an association of theatrelovers and unites those, professional and amateur alike, who desire to support the Living Theatre. Its membership includes the National Theatre, the Royal Shakespeare Theatre, West End managements and British Actors Equity; distinguished scholars, dramatic critics, leading actors, and most Repertory Companies; amateur dramatic societies here and abroad — in banks and schools, universities and community centres, industry and commerce, youth clubs, Women's Institutes and Townswomen's Guilds, hospitals and prisons, and the armed services of the Crown. The BBC and major ITV companies are members of the Association, as are also many public libraries, education authorities and youth committees.

The Association has always been active in campaigning for matters of national importance to the Theatre — the preservation of famous theatre buildings, the National Theatre, the abolition of Entertainments Duty. It has secured recognition for drama as an essential factor in education, is in the forefront of new ideas and trends in the theatre and is particularly concerned in protecting the interest of its members and member groups. It works in association with the Theatres' Advisory Council, which is housed in the Association's premises at Fitzroy Square.

List of Organizations at BTA Headquarters
Association of British Theatre Technicians.
British Children's Theatre Association.
National Council of Theatre for Young People.
Society of Theatre Consultants.
Theatres' Advisory Council.

Organizations Using BTA Headquarters as Accommodation Address.
National Association of Drama Advisers.
Little Theatre Guild of Great Britain.

The National Association of Drama Advisers
The National Association of Drama Advisers was formed in 1960. Its policy is to serve its members by keeping them informed of national developments and by providing national courses. To this end the Association is represented on a number of other bodies, including the Council of Regional Theatres, the National Council of Theatre for Young People, the British Theatre Association, the Drama Board and the National Conference.

The majority of the Association's members are officers to local education authorities, and although there are variations in their individual responsibilities they are generally concerned with the development of drama at child, youth and adult levels. Much of a drama adviser's time is taken up in schools, where he is primarily concerned with the educational applications of drama. This section of his or her work steadily increases as creative drama becomes more and more an integral part of the school curriculum.

In youth and adult areas, drama advisers work towards the improvement of standards of theatre as an art form, and to this end they are available to advise on all aspects of theatrecraft. In addition, they organize or direct courses to cater for all levels of experience, often in the form of youth and adult theatre workshops. A direct result of their efforts in this field is the increasing number of drama centres that are appearing in various parts of the country. These are usually in the form of fully equipped studios, which facilitate experiment by all who wish to further their art. The provision of such facilities and expertise can be of considerable help to any group that wishes to develop its resources.

Most County and some County Borough Education Authorities possess a drama adviser. If you are in any doubt of the existence of one in your area, contact your local education office, or write to: The Secretary, NADA, British Theatre Centre, 9/10 Fitzroy Square, London W1P 6AE.

Index